The American Presi

By CL Gam

For Colby Jones and the students, teachers and employees of the Macon County School District, Lafayette, Tennessee

Table of Contents

Introduction

This book is a brief, simple little volume that provides basic biographical information about America's Presidents from George Washington to Donald Trump. In addition, it provides some interesting and fun facts about each of the Presidents. Each chapter heading lists the President covered by his full name, which may not be the name by which Americans know him best.

This book also contains a brief rundown of each presidential election from 1789 through 2016. However, numbers do not bog it down.

The last section of the book consists of comparative data concerning the Presidents.

This book is not was not written specifically for children. However, it is an easy read and children should be able to enjoy it without difficulty. Adults can perhaps learn a little about America's Chief Executives as well.

It is the hope of the author that this book will spark the interest in readers to learn more about American history in general and in the history of the Presidents of the United States specifically.

The author encourages readers to email him at clgammon@hotmail.com with suggestions, comments, or questions.

About Presidential Elections

Under the American system, each state chooses a number of members to the Electoral

College equal to that state's total number of Unites States Senators and representatives in the Unites States House. The Electoral College then elects the President. However, the members of the Electoral College never come together at a single location. Instead, they meet in their respective state capitals and cast "electoral votes". The candidate with the greatest number of electoral votes – provided it is a majority of the total – becomes President.

If no candidate receives a majority of electoral votes, then the US House of Representatives elects the President. The House chooses from among the top three candidates in the Electoral College vote. In selecting the President, each state has one vote.

National popular vote tallies have no effect on presidential elections. Yet, they provide interesting insights into presidential elections. Records of popular vote totals before 1824 are scant and many states did not choose Electoral College members by popular vote. This being the case, the author did not include any popular vote totals cast prior to 1824.

George Washington

DATE OF BIRTH: February 22, 1732

PLACE OF BIRTH: Pope's Creek, Westmorland County, Virginia

COLLEGE: None

PROFESSIONS: Surveyor, Planter, Soldier

POLITICAL PARTY: Federalist

STATE REPRESENTED: Virginia

OTHER SERVICE: Virginia militia, Commander-in-Chief Continental Army, United States Army (General of the Armies), Justice of the Peace (1760-1774), Virginia House of Burgesses (1758-1774), Continental Congress (1774-1775), President of the Federal Constitutional Convention (1787)

TERM AS PRESIDENT: April 30, 1789-March 3, 1797 (7 years, 308 days)

AGE AT INAUGURATION: 57 years, 67 days

VICE PRESIDENT: John Adams (1789-1797)

OCCUPATION AFTER TERM: Planter, Soldier

LIVED AFTER TERM: 2 years, 285 days

DATE OF DEATH: December 14, 1799

AGE AT DEATH: 67 years, 295 days

PLACE OF DEATH: Mount Vernon, Virginia

PLACE OF BURIAL: Mount Vernon, Virginia

SOME FACTS ABOUT WASHINGTON:

Washington was the first President of the United States.

Washington is the only person to win a presidential election by unanimous vote. Every Electoral College member voted for him in 1789 and 1792.

Washington was the first President to win consecutive presidential elections.

Washington was the first President inaugurated in New York City (first inauguration).

Washington was the first President inaugurated in Philadelphia (second inauguration).

Washington did not serve two full terms. His first term was 57 days short because Congress did not assemble at the appointed time to count the vote of the Electoral College.

Washington was the first President to refuse to seek a third term.

Washington received two electoral votes in 1792 even though he was not a candidate for the presidency.

Washington was the first former General to become President.

Washington was Commander-in-Chief of the United States Army during the Revolutionary War.

Washington was the first President who had signed the United States Constitution.

Washington was the first President born in Virginia.

Washington was the first President born in Westmoreland County, Virginia.

Washington was the first President to represent Virginia.

Washington is the only President who never resided at Washington, D. C.

While Washington never endorsed any political party officially, he aligned himself with the Federalists. Thus, he was the first Federalist President of the United States.

Washington was the first President who had served in the Continental Congress.

Washington was the first President to have a national capital named after him.

Washington unsuccessfully sought election to the Virginia House of Burgesses in 1757.

Washington was the only President to die in the eighteenth century.

Washington was the first President to die in Virginia.

ELECTION OF 1789

George Washington (no party): 69 electoral votes (elected President – See notes below)

John Adams (no party): 34 electoral votes (elected Vice President)

John Jay (no party): 9 electoral votes

Robert Harrison (no party): 6

Others: 20 electoral votes

Note 1: In 1789, each elector cast votes for two candidates for President. The candidate with the most votes became President and the second place candidate became Vice President. In 1789 and 1792, George received one vote from every elector and thus won election unanimously. Since 1800, electors have cast one vote for President and one vote for Vice President.

Note 2: Three states (New York, North Carolina, and Rhode Island) did not take part in the 1789 election.

ELECTION OF 1792

George Washington (Federalist): 132 electoral votes (reelected President)

John Adams (Federalist): 77 electoral votes (reelected Vice President)

George Clinton (Democratic-Republican): 50 electoral votes

Thomas Jefferson (Democratic-Republican): 4 electoral votes

Aaron Burr (Democratic Republican) 1 electoral vote (See note below)

Note: Of the 5 persons receiving electoral votes in 1792, 3 eventually became President and 4 eventually became Vice President.

John Adams

DATE OF BIRTH: October 30, 1735

PLACE OF BIRTH: Braintree (now Quincy) Massachusetts

COLLEGE: Harvard, graduated in 1755

PROFESSION: Lawyer

POLITICAL PARTY: Federalist

STATE REPRESENTED: Massachusetts

OTHER SERVICE: Massachusetts General Court (1768), Continental Congress (1774-1777), American Board of War (1775), Minister to France (1778-1779), Minister to Holland (1780-1782), Minister to England (1785-1788), Vice President of the United States (1789-1797)

TERM AS PRESIDENT: March 4, 1797-March 3, 1801 (4 years)

AGE AT INAUGURATION: 61 years, 125 days

VICE PRESIDENT: Thomas Jefferson (1797-1801)

OCCUPATION AFTER TERM: Author

LIVED AFTER TERM: 25 years, 122 days

DATE OF DEATH: July 4, 1826

AGE AT DEATH: 90 years, 247 days

PLACE OF DEATH: Quincy, Massachusetts

PLACE OF BURIAL: Hancock Cemetery, Quincy, Massachusetts – reinterred at United First Parish Church, Quincy Massachusetts

SOME FACTS ABOUT ADAMS:

Adams was the second President of the United States.

Adams won the election of 1796.

Adams was the first Vice President of the United States.

Adams was the first sitting Vice President to win election to the office of President.

Adams was the first President born in Braintree (now Quincy) Massachusetts.

Adams was the first President to represent Massachusetts.

Adams was the first President to die in Massachusetts.

Adams was the first President with a college degree.

Adams was the first President to serve with a Vice President of a different political party. Adams was a Federalist and Thomas Jefferson was a Democratic-Republican.

Adams was the first sitting President to lose his bid for reelection.

Adams was the first President to reside at the White House.

Adams was the first person to receive electoral votes in four consecutive elections.

Adams was the first former President to have a son (John Quincy Adams) elected President.

Adams nominated George Washington for the post of Commander-in-Chief of the Continental Army in 1775.

Adams was America's first Minister to England.

Adams died the same day as Thomas Jefferson.

Adams was the first President who had signed the Declaration of Independence.

Adams was the first former Ambassador to become President.

Adams was the first President with a law license.

Adams was the first President buried at the United First Parish Church in Quincy Massachusetts.

ELECTION OF 1796

John Adams (Federalist): 71 electoral votes (elected President)

Thomas Jefferson (Democratic-Republican): 68 electoral votes (elected Vice President)

Thomas Pinckney (Federalist): 59 electoral votes

Aaron Burr (Democratic-Republican): 30 electoral votes

Others: 48 electoral votes

Thomas Jefferson

DATE OF BIRTH: April 13, 1743

PLACE OF BIRTH: Shadwell, Goochland County (now Albemarle County), Virginia

COLLEGE: William and Mary, graduated in 1762

PROFESSIONS: Lawyer, Author

POLITICAL PARTY: Democratic-Republican

STATE REPRESENTED: Virginia

OTHER SERVICE: Virginia militia (Colonel), Virginia Colonial House of Burgesses (1769-1775), Continental Congress (1775-1776, 1783-1784), Governor of Virginia (1779-1781), Virginia State House of Delegates (1782), Minister to France (1784-1788), Secretary of State (1789-1793), Vice President (1797-1801)

TERM AS PRESIDENT: March 4, 1801-March 3, 1809 (8 years)

AGE AT INAUGURATION: 57 years, 325 days

VICE PRESIDENTS: Aaron Burr (1801-1805), George Clinton (1805-1809)

OCCUPATION AFTER TERM: Retired

LIVED AFTER TERM: 17 years, 122 days

DATE OF DEATH: July 4, 1826

AGE AT DEATH: 83 years, 82 days

PLACE OF DEATH: Charlottesville, Virginia

PLACE OF BURIAL: Monticello Graveyard, near Charlottesville, Virginia

SOME FACTS ABOUT JEFFERSON:

Jefferson was the third President of the United States.

Jefferson won the presidential elections of 1800 and 1804.

Jefferson was the second Vice President of the United States.

Jefferson was the first President chosen by the United States House of Representatives. In the election of 1800, Jefferson and Aaron Burr tied in the Electoral College vote. The House elected Jefferson on the thirty-sixth ballot.

Jefferson was the first President inaugurated in Washington, D. C.

Jefferson was the first President to have two Vice Presidents.

Jefferson was the first President to serve for eight years.

Jefferson was the first President to graduate from William and Mary University.

Jefferson received electoral votes in four consecutive elections.

Jefferson was the first President who had served in a presidential Cabinet.

Jefferson was the first President who had served as Secretary of State.

Jefferson was the first President who had served as a Governor.

Jefferson chaired the Congressional Committee tasked to construct the Declaration of Independence.

Jefferson was the primary author of the Declaration of Independence.

Jefferson signed the Declaration of Independence.

Jefferson was the first Democratic-Republican President (sometimes called "Republican").

ELECTION OF 1800

Thomas Jefferson (Democratic-Republican): 73 electoral votes (elected President – See note below)

Aaron Burr (Democratic-Republican): 73 electoral votes (elected Vice President)

John Adams (Federalist): 65 electoral votes

Charles Pinckney (Federalist): 64 electoral votes

John Jay: 1 electoral vote

Note: Since Jefferson and Burr tied in the Electoral College, the election fell to the US House of Representatives. Jefferson won in the US House on the thirty-sixth ballot by a vote of 10 states to 4 states for Burr, with 2 states not voting. Thus, Jefferson became President and Burr became Vice President.

ELECTION OF 1804

Thomas Jefferson (Democratic-Republican): 162 electoral votes (reelected President)

Charles Pinckney (Federalist): 14 electoral votes

James Madison, Jr.

KNOWN AS: James Madison

DATE OF BIRTH: March 16, 1751

PLACE OF BIRTH: Port Conway, Virginia

COLLEGE: College of New Jersey (now Princeton), graduated in 1771

PROFESSION: Lawyer

POLITICAL PARTY: Democratic-Republican

STATE REPRESENTED: Virginia

OTHER SERVICE: Virginia militia (Colonel), Committee of Safety for Orange County Virginia (1774), First General Assembly of Virginia (1776), Executive Council (1778), Continental Congress (1780-1783, 1787-1788), Virginia legislature (1884-1886), Federal Constitutional Convention (1787), United States House of Representatives (1789-1797), Secretary of State (1801-1809)

TERM AS PRESIDENT: March 4, 1809-March 3, 1817 (8 years)

AGE AT INAUGURATION: 57 years, 353 days

VICE PRESIDENTS George Clinton (1809-1812), Elbridge Gerry (1813-1814)

OCCUPATION AFTER TERM: Retired

LIVED AFTER TERM: 19 years, 116 days

DATE OF DEATH: June 28, 1836

AGE AT DEATH: 85 years, 104 days

PLACE OF DEATH: Montpelier, Virginia

PLACE OF BURIAL: Family plot, Montpelier, Virginia

SOME FACTS ABOUT MADISON:

Madison was the fourth President of the United States.

Madison won the presidential elections of 1808 and 1812.

Madison was the first person to receive electoral votes for President and Vice President in the same election (1808).

Both of Madison's Vice Presidents died in office. George Clinton died in office on April 20, 1812. Elbridge Gerry died in office on November 23, 1814.

Madison was the first President to serve without a Vice President. He served without a Vice President from April 20, 1812 to March 4, 1813 and from November 23, 1814 to March 4, 1817.

Madison is the only sitting President to exercise his position as Commander-in-Chief as a field commander. He led troops during the War of 1812.

Madison fled Washington, D. C. in August 1814, to avoid the advancing British Army. Madison's wife, Dolly, saved many important documents during their hasty departure.

Madison was the first President who had served in the US House of Representatives.

Madison was the last surviving signer of the US Constitution.

James Madison defeated future President James Monroe for a seat in the first US Congress in 1789. Years later, Madison named Monroe to his Cabinet.

ELECTION OF 1808

James Madison (Democratic-Republican): 122 electoral votes (elected President)

Charles Pinckney (Federalist): 47 electoral votes

George Clinton (Democratic-Republican): 6 electoral votes

ELECTION OF 1812

James Madison (Democratic Republican): 128 electoral votes (reelected President)

DeWitt Clinton (Federalist): 89 electoral votes

James Monroe

DATE OF BIRTH: April 28, 1758

PLACE OF BIRTH: Westmoreland County, Virginia

COLLEGE: William and Mary, graduated in 1776

PROFESSION: Lawyer

POLITICAL PARTY: Democratic-Republican

STATE REPRESENTED: Virginia

OTHER SERVICE: Continental Army (Major), Virginia State Assembly (1782, 1786), Continental Congress (1783-1786), Virginia Convention to consider the Federal Constitution (1788), United States Senate (1790-1794), Minister to France (1794-1796, 1803), Governor of Virginia (1799-1802, 1811), Minister to England (1803-1807), Virginia State Assembly (1810-1811), Secretary of State (1811-1817), Secretary of War (1814-1815), President of the Virginia Constitutional Convention (1829)

TERM AS PRESIDENT: March 4, 1817-March 3, 1825 (8 years)

AGE AT INAUGURATION: 58 years, 310 days

VICE PRESIDENT: Daniel D. Tompkins (1817-1825)

OCCUPATION AFTER TERM: Author

LIVED AFTER TERM: 6 years, 122 days

DATE OF DEATH: July 4, 1831

AGE AT DEATH: 73 years, 67 days

PLACE OF DEATH: New York, New York

PLACE OF BURIAL: Marble Cemetery, New York, New York – reinterred in the Hollywood Cemetery, Richmond, Virginia in 1858

SOME FACTS ABOUT MONROE:

Monroe was the fifth President of the United States.

Monroe won the presidential elections of 1816 and 1820.

Monroe was the only President to suffer wounds during the American Revolution.

Monroe was the first President who had served in the United States Senate.

Monroe was the last President who had served in the Continental Congress.

Monroe was the first President who had served as Secretary of War.

Monroe ran unopposed for President in 1820. He received all but one electoral vote.

Monroe unsuccessfully sought a seat in Congress in 1789.

Monroe had a national capital named after him (Monrovia, Liberia, founded in 1822).

Monroe was the first President to die in New York.

Monroe was the first President buried in the Hollywood Cemetery in Richmond, Virginia.

ELECTION OF 1816

James Monroe (Democratic-Republican): 183 electoral votes (elected President)

Rufus King (Federalist) 34 electoral votes (See note below)

Note: 1816 marked the last year the Federalists fielded a candidate for President.

ELECTION OF 1820

James Monroe (Democratic-Republican): 231 electoral votes (reelected President – See note below)

John Quincy Adams (Democratic-Republican): 1 electoral vote

Note: Monroe ran unopposed for President in 1820. However, one elector from New Hampshire voted for Secretary of State John Quincy Adams.

John Quincy Adams

DATE OF BIRTH: July 11, 1767

PLACE OF BIRTH: Braintree (now Quincy), Massachusetts

COLLEGE: Harvard, graduated in 1787

PROFESSION: Lawyer

POLITICAL PARTY: Republican (aka Democratic-Republican)

STATE REPRESENTED: Massachusetts

OTHER SERVICE: Minister to the Netherlands (1794), Minister to Portugal (1796), Minister to Prussia (1797-1801), Massachusetts State Senate (1802), United States Senate (1803-1808), Minister to Russia (1809-1814), Minister to England (1815-1817), Secretary of State (1817-1825), Member of the US House of Representatives (1831-1848)

TERM AS PRESIDENT: March 4, 1825-March 3, 1829 (4 years)

AGE AT INAUGURATION: 57 years, 236 days

VICE PRESIDENT: John C. Calhoun (1825-1829)

OCCUPATION AFTER TERM: Politics

LIVED AFTER TERM: 18 years, 356 days

DATE OF DEATH: February 23, 1848

AGE AT DEATH: 80 years, 227 days

PLACE OF DEATH: Washington, D. C.

PLACE OF BURIAL: First Unitarian Church, Quincy Massachusetts

SOME FACTS ABOUT ADAMS:

Adams was the sixth President of the United States.

Adams won the presidential election of 1824.

In 1824, the US House of Representatives chose Adams as President over Andrew Jackson and William Crawford on the first ballot. Adams received the votes of 13 states, Jackson picked up 11, and Crawford captured the votes of 4 states.

Adams was the first President who had not served in the Continental Congress.

Adams was the first President whose father had served as President.

Adams was the first President whose father had signed the Declaration of Independence.

Adams was the first President to finish second in the popular vote count and still win the presidency.

Adams was the first President to finish second in the Electoral College vote and still win the presidency.

Adams received the lowest popular percentage of any person elected President.

Adams was the first President to have his photograph taken.

Adams was the National Republican Party nominee for President in 1828. He was the first nominee of the National Republican Party.

Adams was the first President who had changed political parties. He switched from the Federalist Party to the Democratic-Republican Party in 1808. In 1834, Adams switched to the Whig Party.

Adams was the first former President to win a seat in Congress.

Adams chaired the US House Committees on Manufactures (1831-1841, 1843-1847), Indian Affairs (1841-1843), and Foreign Affairs (1841-1843)

Adams was the first President to serve in both the US House and the US Senate.

Adams was an unsuccessful candidate for the US House in 1802.

Adams declined an appointment to the United States Supreme Court in 1811.

Adams was an unsuccessful candidate for Governor of Massachusetts on the Anti-Masonic ticket in 1834.

Adams was the first President to die in Washington, D C.

ELECTION OF 1824

John Quincy Adams (Democratic-Republican): 84 electoral votes, 113,142 popular votes (elected President – See note below)

Andrew Jackson (Democratic-Republican): 99 electoral votes, 151,363 popular votes

William Crawford (Democratic-Republican): 41 electoral votes, 41,032 popular votes

Henry Clay (Democratic-Republican): 37 electoral votes, 47,545 popular votes

Others: 0 electoral votes, 12,846 popular votes

Note: Since no candidate received a majority in the Electoral College, the decision of electing a President fell to the US House of Representatives. The House elected Adams with 13 states, to 7 for Jackson, and with 4 going for Crawford.

Andrew Jackson

DATE OF BIRTH: March 15, 1767

PLACE OF BIRTH: Waxhaw, South Carolina

COLLEGE: None

PROFESSION: Soldier, Planter, Merchant, Lawyer

POLITICAL PARTY: Democratic

STATE REPRESENTED: Tennessee

OTHER SERVICE: Tennessee Militia, Continental Army, US Army (Major General), Solicitor of the Western District of North Carolina (later of the territory which became Tennessee) (1788-1791), United States House of Representatives (1796-1797), US Senate (1797-1798, 1823-1825), Tennessee State Supreme Court (1798-1804), Governor of the Florida Territory (1821)

TERM AS PRESIDENT: March 4, 1829-March 3, 1837 (8 years)

AGE AT INAUGURATION: 61 years, 354 days

VICE PRESIDENTS: John C. Calhoun (1829-1832), Martin Van Buren (1833-1837)

OCCUPATION AFTER TERM: Planter

LIVED AFTER TERM: 8 years, 96 days

DATE OF DEATH: June 8, 1845

AGE AT DEATH: 78 years, 85 days

PLACE OF DEATH: Nashville, Tennessee

PLACE OF BURIAL: The Hermitage Estate, Nashville, Tennessee

SOME FACTS ABOUT JACKSON:

Jackson was the seventh President of the United States.

Jackson won the presidential elections of 1828 and 1832.

Jackson was the first President born in a log cabin.

Jackson was the first President born in South Carolina.

Jackson was the first President to represent Tennessee.

Jackson was the first President who represented a state other than the state of his birth.

Jackson was the first President to die in Tennessee.

Jackson was an unsuccessful candidate for President in 1824.

Jackson was the first person to receive a plurality of the popular vote, but fail to win the election (1824).

Jackson was the first person to receive a plurality of the electoral vote, but fail to win the election (1824).

Jackson was the first President to receive his party's nomination at a national convention.

Jackson popularized the term "Democratic Party" and was the first Democratic President.

Jackson was the first person to receive a plurality of the popular vote on three separate occasions. He was also the first person to receive a plurality of the electoral vote thrice.

Jackson served from December 28, 1832 to March 3, 1833 without a Vice President. Vice President John C. Calhoun resigned on December 28, 1832.

Jackson chaired the US Senate Committee on Military Affairs (1823-1825).

Jackson was the first President who had served as a Justice of a state Supreme Court.

ELECTION OF 1828

Andrew Jackson (Democratic): 178 electoral votes, 642,806 popular votes (elected President)

John Quincy Adams (National Republican: 83 electoral votes, 501,967 popular votes

Others: 0 electoral votes, 4,443 popular votes

ELECTION OF 1832

Andrew Jackson (Democratic): 219 electoral votes, 702,735 popular votes (reelected President)

Henry Clay (National Republican): 49 electoral votes, 474,107 popular votes

John Floyd (Independent Democrat): 11 electoral votes, 0 popular votes

William Wirt (Anti-Masonic): 7 electoral votes, 99,817 popular votes

Others: 0 electoral votes, 7,061 popular votes

Martin Van Buren

DATE OF BIRTH: December 5, 1782

PLACE OF BIRTH: Kinderhook, New York

COLLEGE: None

PROFESSION: Lawyer

POLITICAL PARTY: Democratic

STATE REPRESENTED: New York

OTHER SERVICE: Surrogate of Columbia County, New York (1808), New York State Senate (1813-1820), New York State Attorney General (1815-1819), US Senate (1821-1828), Governor of New York (1829), US Secretary of State (1829-1831), Minister to Great Britain (1831-1832), Vice President (1833-1837)

TERM AS PRESIDENT: March 4, 1837-March 3, 1841 (4 years)

AGE AT INAUGURATION: 54 years, 89 days

VICE PRESIDENT: Richard M. Johnson (1837-1841)

OCCUPATION AFTER TERM: Politics, Retired

LIVED AFTER TERM: 21 years, 142 days

DATE OF DEATH: July 24, 1862

AGE AT DEATH: 79 years, 231 days

PLACE OF DEATH: Kinderhook, New York

PLACE OF BURIAL: Kinderhook Cemetery, Kinderhook, New York

SOME FACTS ABOUT VAN BUREN:

Van Buren was the eighth President of the United States.

Van Buren won the presidential election of 1836.

Van Buren was the eighth Vice President of the United States.

Van Buren was the first President born in New York.

Van Buren was the first President to Represent New York.

Van Buren was the first President born a citizen of the United States.

Van Buren chaired the US Senate Committee on the Judiciary (1823-1828).

Van Buren received the most votes on the first ballot at the 1844 Democratic National Convention, but not enough to win the nomination. James K. Polk secured the nomination on the ninth ballot.

Van Buren was the first former President to seek election as President on a third-party ticket. In 1848, Van Buren ran for President on the Free Soil ticket. He finished third.

Van Buren received nine electoral votes for Vice President in 1824. John C. Calhoun won the election for Vice President.

ELECTION OF 1836

Martin Van Buren (Democratic): 170 electoral votes, 763,291 popular votes (elected President)

William Henry Harrison (Whig): 73 electoral votes, 549,907 popular votes

Hugh White (Whig): 26 electoral votes, 146,107 popular votes

Daniel Webster (Whig): 14 electoral votes, 41,201 popular votes

Others: 11 electoral votes, 2,305 popular votes (See note)

Note: The South Carolina legislature awarded Willie Mangum the state's 11 electoral votes. South Carolina voters did not elect their members of the Electoral College until after the Civil War.

William Henry Harrison

DATE OF BIRTH: February 9, 1773

PLACE OF BIRTH: Berkeley, Charles City County, Virginia

COLLEGE: Hampden-Sidney College and University of Pennsylvania, did not graduate from either

PROFESSIONS: Solider

POLITICAL PARTY: Whig

STATE REPRESENTED: Ohio

OTHER SERVICE: United States Army (Major General), Secretary of the Northwest Territory (1798-1799), US House of Representatives (1799-1800, 1816-1819), Territorial Governor of Indiana (1800-1813), Ohio State Senate (1819-1821), US Senate (1825-1828), Minister to Columbia (1828-1829)

TERM AS PRESIDENT: March 4, 1841-April 4, 1841 (32 days)

AGE AT INAUGURATION: 68 years, 23 days

VICE PRESIDENT: John Tyler (1841)

LIVED AFTER TERM: Died in Office

DATE OF DEATH: April 4, 1841

AGE AT DEATH: 68 years, 54 days

PLACE OF DEATH: Washington, D. C.

PLACE OF BURIAL: Harrison Tomb, North Bend, Ohio

SOME FACTS ABOUT HARRISON:

Harrison was the ninth President of the United States.

Harrison won the presidential election of 1840.

Harrison was the first Whig President.

Harrison was the first President to die in office.

Harrison served the shortest period in office of any President (32 days).

Harrison was the last President born a British subject.

Harrison was the first President to represent Ohio.

Harrison was the first President to have a grandchild elected President (Benjamin Harrison).

Harrison was born in the same county as his Vice President, John Tyler.

Harrison chaired the US Senate Committee on Military Affairs (1825-1828).

ELECTION OF 1840

William Henry Harrison (Whig): 234 electoral votes, 1,275,583 popular votes (elected President)

Martin Van Buren (Democratic): 60 electoral votes, 1,129,645 popular votes

James G. Birney (Liberty): 0 electoral votes, 7,453 popular votes

Others: 0 electoral votes, 13 popular votes

John Tyler

DATE OF BIRTH: March 29, 1790

PLACE OF BIRTH: Charles City County, Virginia

COLLEGE: William an Mary, graduated in 1807

PROFESSION: Lawyer

POLITICAL PARTY: Whig

STATE REPRESENTED: Virginia

OTHER SERVICE: Virginia Militia (Captain), Virginia House of Delegates (1811-1816, 1823-1825, and 1839) Virginia Counsel of State (1816), US House of Representatives (1817-1821), Governor of Virginia (1825-1827), US Senate (1827-1836), Virginia Constitutional Convention (1829, 1830), President pro tempore of the United States Senate (1835-1836), Vice President (1841), Virginia secession convention (1861), Confederate Provisional Congress (1861)

TERM AS PRESIDENT: April 4, 1841-March 3, 1845 (3 years, 332 days)

AGE AT INAUGURATION: 51 years, 8 days

VICE PRESIDENT: None

OCCUPATION AFTER TERM: Lawyer

LIVED AFTER TERM: 16 years, 320 days

DATE OF DEATH: January 18, 1862

AGE AT DEATH: 71 years, 295 days

PLACE OF DEATH: Richmond, Virginia

PLACE OF BURIAL: Hollywood Cemetery, Richmond, Virginia

SOME FACTS ABOUT TYLER

Tyler was the tenth President of the United States.

Tyler was the tenth Vice President of the United States.

Tyler was the first Vice President to become Chief Executive upon the death a President.

Tyler was the first President to serve his entire term without a Vice President.

Tyler was the first President who never won presidential election.

Tyler was the first President who married while in office.

Tyler was the first President whose father had served as a state Governor.

Tyler was an unsuccessful candidate for Vice President in 1836.

In 1843, several members of the US House of Representatives brought articles of impeachment against Tyler. The impeachment effort failed.

Tyler threatened to run for reelection on a third-party ticket (National Democratic Party) in 1844, but he eventually withdrew.

In 1845, Tyler was the first President to have a veto overridden.

Tyler was the first President who had served as President pro tempore of the US Senate.

Tyler chaired the US Senate committees on the District of Columbia (1833-1836) and Manufactures (1833-1835).

Tyler won election to the Confederate House of Representatives in 1862, but died before taking office.

President Lincoln broke precedent when he took made no official notice of Tyler's passing.

Tyler entered college at the age of twelve.

Tyler was the first President born after the end of the American Revolution.

James Knox Polk

KNOWN AS: James K. Polk

DATE OF BIRTH: November 2, 1795

PLACE OF BIRTH: Mecklenburg County, North Carolina

COLLEGE: University of North Carolina, graduated in 1818

PROFESSION: Lawyer

POLITICAL PARTY: Democratic

STATE REPRESENTED: Tennessee

OTHER SERVICE: Tennessee Militia (Colonel), Chief Clerk of the Tennessee State Senate (1821-1823), Tennessee State House of Representatives (1823-1825), US House of Representatives (1825-1839), Speaker of the US House of Representative (1835-1839), Governor of Tennessee (1839-1841)

TERM AS PRESIDENT: March 4, 1845-March 3, 1849 (4 years)

AGE AT INAUGURATION: 49 years, 122 days

VICE PRESIDENT: George M. Dallas (1845-1849)

OCCUPATION AFTER TERM: retired

LIVED AFTER TERM: 103 days

DATE OF DEATH: June 15, 1849

AGE AT DEATH: 53 years, 225 days

PLACE OF DEATH: Nashville, Tennessee

PLACE OF BURIAL: Polk Place, Nashville, Tennessee – reinterred at the State Capitol Grounds, Nashville, Tennessee

SOME FACTS ABOUT POLK:

Polk was the eleventh President of the United States.

Polk won the presidential election of 1844.

Polk was the first President born in North Carolina.

Polk was the first President who had served as Speaker of the US House of Representatives.

Polk chaired the US House Ways and Means Committee (1833-1835).

Polk received one electoral vote for Vice President in 1840.

ELECTION OF 1844

James K. Polk (Democratic): 170 electoral votes, 1,339,570 popular votes (elected President)

Henry Clay (Whig): 105 electoral votes, 1,300,157 popular votes

James G. Birney (Liberty): 0 electoral votes, 62,054 popular votes

Others: 0 electoral votes, 2,083

Zachary Taylor

DATE OF BIRTH: November 24, 1784

PLACE OF BIRTH: Montebello, Orange County, Virginia

COLLEGE: None

PROFESSION: Soldier

POLITICAL PARTY: Whig

STATE REPRESENTED: Louisiana

OTHER SERVICE: US Army (Major General)

TERM AS PRESIDENT: March 4, 1849-July 9, 1850 (1 year, 127 days)

AGE AT INAUGURATION: 64 years, 100 days

VICE PRESIDENT: Millard Fillmore (1849-1850)

LIVED AFTER TERM: Died in Office

DATE OF DEATH: July 9, 1850

AGE AT DEATH: 65 years, 227, days

PLACE OF DEATH: Washington, D. C.

PLACE OF BURIAL: Congressional Cemetery, Washington D. C. – reinterred at the Zachary Taylor National Cemetery, Louisville, Kentucky

SOME FACTS ABOUT TAYLOR:

Taylor was the twelfth President of the United States.

Taylor won the presidential election of 1848.

Taylor was the first President who never served in either the US Congress or the Continental Congress.

Taylor was the first President to represent Louisiana.

Taylor never sought elective office before winning the presidential election of 1848.

Taylor was a career solider. He won the presidential election on November 7, 1848, but he did not resign from the Army until January 31, 1849.

ELECTION OF 1848

Zachary Taylor (Whig): 163 electoral votes, 1,360,235 popular votes (elected President)

Lewis Cass (Democratic): 127 electoral votes, 1,222,353 popular votes

Martin Van Buren (Free Soil): 0 electoral votes, 291,475 popular votes

Others: 0 electoral votes, 2,755 popular votes

Millard Fillmore

DATE OF BIRTH: January 7, 1800

PLACE OF BIRTH: Locke Township (now Summerhill), Cayuga County, New York

COLLEGE: None

PROFESSION: Lawyer

POLITICAL PARTY: Whig

STATE REPRESENTED: New York

OTHER SERVICE: New York State Militia (Major), New York State Assembly (1829-1831), US House of Representatives (1833-1835, 1837-1843), New York State Comptroller (1847-1849), Vice President (1849-1850)

TERM AS PRESIDENT: July 10, 1850-March 3, 1853 (2 years, 236 days)

AGE AT INAUGURATION: 50 years, 184 days

VICE PRESIDENT: None

OCCUPATION AFTER TERM: Politics, Presidential Candidate, Chancellor of the University of Buffalo

LIVED AFTER TERM: 21 years, 4 days

DATE OF DEATH: March 8, 1874

AGE AT DEATH: 74 years, 60 days

PLACE OF DEATH: Buffalo, New York

PLACE OF BURIAL: Forest Lawn Cemetery, Buffalo, New York

SOME FACTS ABOUT FILLMORE:

Fillmore was the thirteenth President of the United States.

Fillmore was the twelfth Vice President of the United States.

Fillmore never won a presidential election.

Fillmore was the unsuccessful Whig nominee for Governor of New York in 1844.

Fillmore was unsuccessful in his efforts to gain the Whig nomination for President in 1852. Fillmore led after the first ballot, and continued to lead for several thereafter. However, he lost the nomination to Winfield Scott on fifty-third ballot.

Fillmore was the presidential nominee of the American and Whig parties in 1856. He finished third in the three-way contest.

Fillmore was the first President born in the Nineteenth Century.

Franklin Pierce

DATE OF BIRTH: November 23, 1804

PLACE OF BIRTH: Hillsborough (now Hillsboro), New Hampshire

COLLEGE: Bowdoin College, graduated in 1824

PROFESSION: Lawyer

POLITICAL PARTY: Democratic

STATE REPRESENTED: New Hampshire

OTHER SERVICE: United States Army (Brigadier General), New York State General Court (1829-1833), Speaker of the York State General Court (1832-1833), US House of Representatives (1833-1837), US Senate (1837-1842), Chair of New Hampshire state constitutional convention (1850)

TERM AS PRESIDENT: March 4, 1853-March 3, 1857 (4 years)

AGE AT INAUGURATION: 48 years, 101 days

VICE PRESIDENT: William Rufus De Vane King (1853)

OCCUPATION AFTER TERM: Retired

LIVED AFTER TERM: 12 years, 218 days

DATE OF DEATH: October 8, 1869

AGE AT DEATH: 64 years, 319 days

PLACE OF DEATH: Concord, New Hampshire

PLACE OF BURIAL: Old North Cemetery, Concord, New Hampshire

SOME FACTS ABOUT PIERCE:

Pierce was the fourteenth President of the United States.

Pierce won the presidential election of 1852.

Pierce was the first President born in New Hampshire.

Pierce was the first President to represent to New Hampshire.

Pierce served from April 18, 1853 to March 3, 1857 without a Vice President due to the death of William Rufus De Vane King.

Pierce made no changes to his Cabinet during his term.

Pierce chaired the US Senate Committee on Pensions (1839-1841).

Pierce is the only elected President to unsuccessfully seek nomination from his party for a second term (1856).

Pierce declined appointment to the office of US Attorney General in 1846.

Pierce "affirmed" rather than swore during his oath of office.

Pierce was the first President to die in New Hampshire.

ELECTION OF 1852

Franklin Pierce (Democratic): 254 electoral votes, 1,605,943 popular votes (elected President)

Winfield Scott (Whig): 42 electoral votes, 1,386,418 popular votes

John Hale (Free Soil): 0 electoral votes, 155,799 popular votes

Others: 0 electoral votes, 11,480 popular votes

James Buchanan

DATE OF BIRTH: April 23, 1791

PLACE OF BIRTH: Cove Gap, Pennsylvania

COLLEGE: Dickinson College, graduated in 1809

PROFESSION: Lawyer

POLITICAL PARTY: Democratic

STATE REPRESENTED: Pennsylvania

OTHER SERVICE: Pennsylvania State Militia (Private), Pennsylvania House of Representatives (1814-1815), US House of Representatives (1821-1831), Justice of the US District Court of Missouri (1832-1834), Minister to Russia, US Senate (1834-1845), Secretary of State (1845-1849), Minister to Great Britain (1853-1856)

TERM AS PRESIDENT: March 4, 1857-March 3, 1861 (4 years)

AGE AT INAUGURATION: 65 years, 315 days

VICE PRESIDENT: John C. Breckinridge (1857-1861)

OCCUPATION AFTER TERM: Author

LIVED AFTER TERM: 7 years, 89 days

DATE OF DEATH: June 1, 1868

AGE AT DEATH: 77 years, 39 days

PLACE OF DEATH: Lancaster, Pennsylvania

PLACE OF BURIAL: Woodward Hill Cemetery, Lancaster, Pennsylvania

SOME FACTS ABOUT BUCHANAN:

Buchanan was the fifteenth President of the United States.

Buchanan won the presidential election of 1856.

Buchanan was the first President born in Pennsylvania.

Buchanan was the first President to represent Pennsylvania.

Buchanan was the only President who never married.

Buchanan chaired the US House Committee on the Judiciary (1829-1831).

Buchanan chaired the US Senate Committee on Foreign Relations (1835-1841).

Buchanan was the last President born in the Eighteenth Century.

Buchanan was the first President to die in Pennsylvania.

ELECTION OF 1856

James Buchanan (Democratic): 174 electoral votes, 1,835,140 popular votes (elected President)

John Fremont (Republican): 114 electoral votes, 1,340,668 popular votes (See note 1 below)

Millard Fillmore (American, Whig) 8 electoral votes, 872,703 popular votes (See note 2 below)

Others: 0 electoral votes, 3,094 popular votes

Note 1: 1856 was the first year in which the Republican Party nominated a candidate for President.

Note 2: 1856 was the last year in which the Whig Party nominated a candidate for President. In addition, 1856 was the only year in which this variation of the American Party nominated a candidate for President.

Abraham Lincoln

DATE OF BIRTH: February 12, 1809

PLACE OF BIRTH: Hodgenville, Hardin (now Larue) County, Kentucky

COLLEGE: None

PROFESSIONS: Lawyer

POLITICAL PARTY: Republican

STATE REPRESENTED: Illinois

OTHER SERVICE: Illinois State Militia (Captain), Illinois State House of Representatives (1834-1840), US House of Representatives (1847-1849)

TERM AS PRESIDENT: March 4, 1861-April 15, 1865 (4 years, 42 days)

AGE AT INAUGURATION: 52 years, 20 days

VICE PRESIDENTS: Hannibal Hamlin (1861-1865), Andrew Johnson (1865)

LIVED AFTER TERM: Died in Office

DATE OF DEATH: April 15, 1865

AGE AT DEATH: 56 years, 62 days

PLACE OF DEATH: Washington, D. C.

PLACE OF BURIAL: Oak Ridge Cemetery, Springfield, Illinois

SOME FACTS ABOUT LINCOLN:

Lincoln was the sixteenth President of the United States.

Lincoln won the presidential elections of 1860 and 1864.

Lincoln was the first Republican President.

Lincoln was the first President to represent Illinois.

Lincoln was the first President assassinated. Confederate sympathizer, John Wilkes Booth shot Lincoln on the evening of April 14, 1865. Lincoln died the next day.

Lincoln was the first President born in Kentucky.

Lincoln was the first President born outside the original thirteen states.

Lincoln sought the Republican nomination for Vice President 1856, but he lost to William L. Dayton.

When Lincoln left the Army in 1832, he held the rank of Private.

Lincoln was the first President who had obtained a patent for an invention.

ELECTION OF 1860

Abraham Lincoln (Republican): 180 electoral votes, 1,855,993 popular votes, (elected President)

John Breckinridge (National Democrat): 72 electoral votes, 851,844 popular votes

John Bell (Constitutional Union): 39 electoral votes, 590,946 popular votes

Stephen Douglas (Democratic): 12 electoral votes, 1,381,944 popular votes

Others: 0 popular votes, 540 popular votes

ELECTION OF 1864

Abraham Lincoln (Republican): 212 electoral votes, 2,211,317 popular votes (reelected President – See note below)

George McClellan (Democratic): 21 electoral votes, 1,806,227 popular votes

Others: 0 electoral votes, 658 popular votes

Note: The eleven states comprising the Confederate States of America did not take part in the election. In addition, 1 elector from, Nevada did not vote.

Andrew Johnson

DATE OF BIRTH: December 29, 1808

PLACE OF BIRTH: Raleigh, North Carolina

COLLEGE: None

PROFESSION: Tailor

POLITICAL PARTY: Republican (aka Union), Johnson returned to the Democratic Party while still serving as President.

STATE REPRESENTED: Tennessee

OTHER SERVICE: US Army (Brigadier General), Alderman of Greeneville, Tennessee (1828-1830), Mayor of Greeneville (1834-1838), Tennessee State House of Representatives (1835-1837, 1839-1841), Tennessee State Senate (1841-1843), US House of Representatives (1843-1853), Governor of Tennessee (1853-1857), US Senate (1857-1862, 1875), Military Governor of Tennessee (1862-1865), Vice President (1865)

TERM AS PRESIDENT: April 15, 1865-March 3, 1869 (3 years, 3 years, 323 days)

AGE AT INAUGURATION: 56 years, 107 days

VICE PRESIDENT: None

OCCUPATION AFTER TERM: Politics

LIVED AFTER TERM: 6 years, 149 days

DATE OF DEATH: July 31, 1875

AGE AT DEATH: 66 years, 214 days

PLACE OF DEATH: Carter's Station, Tennessee

PLACE OF BURIAL: Andrew Johnson National Cemetery, Greeneville, Tennessee

SOME FACTS ABOUT JOHNSON

Johnson was the seventeenth President of the United States.

Johnson was the sixteenth Vice President of the United States.

Johnson never won a presidential election.

Johnson was the first President to assume the office due to assassination of his predecessor.

Johnson was the first President who had served as a Mayor.

Johnson was the first President who had neither a legal nor a military background.

Johnson chaired the US House Committee on Public Expenditures (1849-1853).

Johnson chaired the US Senate Committee to Audit and Control the Contingent Expenses (1859-1861) and the Committee on the District of Columbia (1859-1861).

Johnson was the first President impeached by the US House of Representatives (1865). The US Senate acquitted him by a single vote.

Johnson unsuccessfully sought the Democratic nomination for President in 1868. He lost to Horatio Seymour.

Johnson was the first former President to win election to the US Senate.

Ulysses Simpson Grant

KNOWN AS: Ulysses S. Grant

DATE OF BIRTH: April 27, 1822

PLACE OF BIRTH: Point Pleasant, Ohio

COLLEGE: United States Military Academy at West Point, New York, graduated in 1843

PROFESSION: Solider, Merchant

POLITICAL PARTY: Republican

STATE REPRESENTED: Illinois

OTHER SERVICE: US Army (General of the Army), Secretary of War (ad interim) (1867-1868)

TERM AS PRESIDENT: March 4, 1869-March 3, 1877 (8 years)

AGE AT INAUGURATION: 46 years, 311 days

VICE PRESIDENTS: Schuyler Colfax (1869-1873), Henry Wilson (1873-1875)

OCCUPATION AFTER TERM: Politics, Author

LIVED AFTER TERM: 8 years, 141 days

DATE OF DEATH: July 23, 1885

AGE AT DEATH: 63 years, 87 days

PLACE OF DEATH: Mount McGregor, New York

PLACE OF BURIAL: Grant's Tomb, New York, New York

SOME FACTS ABOUT GRANT

Grant was the eighteenth President of the United States.

Grant won the presidential elections of 1868 and 1872.

Grant was born with the name Hiram Ulysses Grant. In 1839, he listed his name Ulysses Hiram Grant on his application to West Point. Someone changed the name during the processing of the application to Ulysses Simpson Grant. Grant never bothered to correct the error.

Grant served from November 22, 1875 to March 3, 1879 without a Vice President due to the death of Henry Wilson.

Grant was the first President born in Ohio.

Grant was the first President to graduate from the United States Military Academy.

Grant had never sought an elective office before seeking the Republican nomination for President in 1864. He lost to President Lincoln.

ELECTION OF 1868

Ulysses S. Grant (Republican): 214 electoral votes, 3,013,790 popular votes (elected President – See notes below)

Horatio Seymour (Democratic): 80 electoral votes, 2,708,980 popular votes

Others: 0 electoral votes, 46 popular votes

Note 1: Three former Confederate states (Virginia, Mississippi, and Texas) did not take part in the 1868 presidential election.

Note 2: The Florida legislature chose that state's Electoral College members in 1868.

ELECTION OF 1872

Ulysses S. Grant (Republican): 286 electoral votes (See note 1 below), 3,597,439 popular votes (reelected President)

Horace Greeley (Democratic, Liberal Republican): 3 electoral votes (See note 2 below), 2,833,710 popular votes

Charles O'Conor (Straight-Out Democrat): 0 electoral votes, 23,054 popular votes

Others: 63 electoral votes, 17,780 popular votes

Note 1: The Democrats disputed the 14 Grant electoral votes from Arkansas and Louisiana and Congress declined to count them.

Note 2: Horace Greeley died before the Electoral College voted. 63 electors he won split between Thomas Hendricks (42), Benjamin G. Brown (18), Charles Jenkins (2), and David Davis (1). Congress did not count the 3 cast for Greeley.

Rutherford Birchard Hayes

KNOWN AS: Rutherford B. Hayes

DATE OF BIRTH: October 4, 1822

PLACE OF BIRTH: Delaware, Ohio

COLLEGE: Kenyon College, graduated in 1842

PROFESSION: Lawyer

POLITICAL PARTY: Republican

STATE REPRESENTED: Ohio

OTHER SERVICE: US Army (Major General), Cincinnati City Solicitor (1857-1859), US House of Representatives (1865-1867), Ohio Governor (1868-1872, 1876-1877)

TERM AS PRESIDENT: March 4, 1877-March 3, 1781 (4 years)

AGE AT INAUGURATION: 54 years, 151 days

VICE PRESIDENT: William A. Wheeler (1877-1881)

OCCUPATION AFTER TERM: Philanthropy

LIVED AFTER TERM: 11 years, 319 days

DATE OF DEATH: January 17, 1893

AGE AT DEATH: 70 years, 105 days

PLACE OF DEATH: Fremont, Ohio

PLACE OF BURIAL: Oakwood Cemetery, Fremont, Ohio – reinterred Spiegel Grove, Fremont, Ohio

SOME FACTS ABOUT HAYES:

Hayes was the nineteenth President of the United States.

Hayes won the presidential election of 1876.

Both major candidates in 1876 disputed the election results in several states. Congress created an Electoral Commission to decide the contests. The commission ruled in favor of Hayes in every contested state. This allowed Hayes to win the election by a single electoral vote.

Hayes ordered the installation of the first telephone in the White House.

Hayes was the first President to die in Ohio.

ELECTION OF 1876

Rutherford B. Hayes (Republican): 185 electoral votes (See note below), 4,034,142 popular votes (elected President)

Samuel Tilden (Democratic): 184 electoral votes, 4,286,808 popular votes

Peter Cooper (Greenback): 0 electoral votes, 83,726 popular votes

Others: 0 electoral votes, 13,983 popular votes

Note: The candidates disputed the election returns in Florida, Louisiana, and South Carolina. In addition, they disputed one electoral vote in Oregon. A special electoral commission settled all the disputes in favor Hayes and he won the election.

James Abram Garfield

KNOWN AS: James A. Garfield

DATE OF BIRTH: November 19, 1831

PLACE OF BIRTH: Orange, Ohio

COLLEGE: Williams College, graduated in 1856

PROFESSION: Teacher

POLITICAL PARTY: Republican

STATE REPRESENTED: Ohio

OTHER SERVICE: US Army (Major General), Ohio State Senate (1859), United States House of Representatives (1863-1880),

TERM AS PRESIDENT: March 4, 1881-September 19, 1881 (199 days)

AGE AT INAUGURATION: 49 years, 105 days

VICE PRESIDENT: Chester A. Arthur (1881)

LIVED AFTER TERM: Died in Office

DATE OF DEATH: September 19, 1881

AGE AT DEATH: 49 years, 304 days

PLACE OF DEATH: Elberon, New Jersey

PLACE OF BURIAL: Lake View Cemetery, Cleveland, Ohio

SOME FACTS ABOUT GARFIELD:

Garfield was the twentieth President of the United States.

Garfield won the presidential election of 1880.

Garfield's full name was James Abram Garfield.

Garfield chaired the US House Committees on Military Affairs (1867-1869), Banking and Currency (1869-1871), and Appropriations (1871-1875).

Garfield sat on the Electoral Commission to decide the contests in various states in the presidential election of 1876. Garfield supported Rutherford B. Hayes in every contest.

Garfield won election to the US Senate in 1880. However, he declined to serve due to his election as President.

Garfield was the first left-handed President.

Garfield died at the hands of an assassination. Charles J. Guiteau was disgruntled because he failed to receive a position in the Garfield administration. He shot Garfield on July 2, 1881 in Washington, D. C. Garfield died on September 19, 1881.

Garfield was the first President to die in New Jersey.

ELECTION OF 1880

James A. Garfield (Republican): 214 electoral votes, 4,453,337 popular votes (elected President)

Winfield Hancock (Democratic): 155 electoral votes, 4,444,267 popular votes

James B. Weaver (Greenback): 0 electoral votes, 306,135 popular votes

Others: 0 electoral votes, 13,671 popular votes

Chester Alan Arthur

KNOWN AS: Chester A. Arthur

DATE OF BIRTH: October 5, 1829

PLACE OF BIRTH: Fairfield, Vermont

COLLEGE: Union College (Schenectady, New York), graduated in 1848

PROFESSION: Teacher, Lawyer

POLITICAL PARTY: Republican

STATE REPRESENTED: New York

OTHER SERVICE: New York State Militia (Brigadier General), Collector of the Port of New York (1871-1878), Vice President (1881)

TERM AS PRESIDENT: September 19, 1881-March 3, 1885 (3 years, 166 days)

AGE AT INAUGURATION: 51 years, 350 days

VICE PRESIDENT: None

OCCUPATION AFTER TERM: Lawyer

LIVED AFTER TERM: 1 year, 260 days

DATE OF DEATH: November 18, 1886

AGE AT DEATH: 57 years, 44 days

PLACE OF DEATH: New York, New York

PLACE OF BURIAL: Albany Rural Cemetery, Menands, New York

SOME FACTS ABOUT ARTHUR:

Arthur was the twenty-first President of the United States.

Arthur never won a presidential election.

Arthur was the twentieth Vice President of the United States.

Arthur was the first President born in Vermont.

Arthur attempted to gain the Republican nomination for President in 1884, but lost to James G. Blaine on the fourth ballot.

Stephen Grover Cleveland

KNOWN AS: Grover Cleveland

DATE OF BIRTH: March 18, 1837

PLACE OF BIRTH: Caldwell, New Jersey

COLLEGE: None

PROFESSIONS: Teacher, Lawyer

POLITICAL PARTY: Democratic

STATE REPRESENTED: New York

OTHER SERVICE: Ward Supervisor, Buffalo, New York (1862), Assistant District Attorney, Erie County, New York (1863-1865), Sheriff, Erie County, New York (1871-1873), Mayor of Buffalo, New York (1882), Governor of New York (1883-1885),

TERMS AS PRESIDENT: March 4, 1885, March 3, 1889 (4 years) March 4, 1893-March 3, 1897 (4 years)

AGES AT INAUGURATION: 47 years, 351 days, 55 years, 351 days

VICE PRESIDENTS: Thomas A. Hendricks (1885), Adlai E. Stevenson (1893-1897)

OCCUPATION AFTER SECOND TERM: Retired

LIVED AFTER SECOND TERM: 11 years, 112 days

DATE OF DEATH: June 24, 1908

AGE AT DEATH: 71 years, 98 days

PLACE OF DEATH: Princeton, New Jersey

PLACE OF BURIAL: Princeton Cemetery, Princeton New Jersey

SOME FACTS ABOUT CLEVELAND:

Cleveland was the twenty-second and twenty-fourth Presidents of the United.

Cleveland won the presidential elections 1884 and 1892.

Cleveland was the first President to serve two non-consecutive terms.

Cleveland was the first President to be married in the White House.

Cleveland served from November 22, 1885 to March 3, 1889 without a Vice President due to the death of Thomas A. Hendricks.

Cleveland was the first President born in New Jersey.

Cleveland was the first President elected after the Civil War who had not taken part in the conflict.

Cleveland was the first member of the Democratic Party elected President after the Civil War.

Cleveland was the first President who had served as a county Sheriff.

Cleveland won a plurality of the popular vote in three presidential elections.

Cleveland won two presidential elections, but never received a majority of the vote.

Cleveland served as a Mayor.

Cleveland executed convicted murderers by hanging as a part of his duties as Sheriff of Erie County, New York.

ELECTION OF 1884

Grover Cleveland (Democratic): 219 electoral votes, 4,914,482 popular votes (elected President)

James Blaine (Republican): 182 electoral votes, 4,856,903 popular votes

John St. John (Prohibition): 0 electoral votes, 150,890 popular votes

Benjamin Butler (Greenback): 0 electoral votes, 134,294 popular votes

Others: 0 electoral votes, 3,576 popular votes

ELECTION OF 1892

Grover Cleveland (Democratic): 277 electoral votes, 5,553,898 popular votes (elected President)

Benjamin Harrison (Republican): 145 electoral votes, 5,190,799 popular votes

James Weaver B. Weaver (Populist): 22 electoral votes, 1,026,595 popular votes

John Bidwell (Prohibition): 0 electoral votes, 270,889 popular votes

Others: 0 electoral votes, 25,846 popular votes

Benjamin Harrison

DATE OF BIRTH: August 20, 1833

PLACE OF BIRTH: North Bend, Ohio

COLLEGE: Miami (Ohio) University, graduated in 1852

PROFESSION: Lawyer

POLITICAL PARTY: Republican

STATE REPRESENTED: Indiana

OTHER SERVICE: US Army (Brigadier General), Reporter of the Indiana Supreme Court (1864-1868), Mississippi River Commission (1879), United States Senate (1881-1887), Attorney for the Republic of Venezuela (1900)

TERM AS PRESIDENT: March 4, 1889-March 3, 1893 (4 years)

AGE AT INAUGURATION: 55 years, 196 days

VICE PRESIDENT: Levi P. Morton (1889-1893)

OCCUPATION AFTER TERM: Lawyer, Teacher

LIVED AFTER TERM: 8 years, 9 days

DATE OF DEATH: March 13, 1901

AGE AT DEATH: 67 years, 205 days

PLACE OF DEATH: Indianapolis, Indiana

PLACE OF BURIAL: Crown Hill Cemetery, Indianapolis, Indiana

SOME FACTS ABOUT HARRISON

Harrison was the twenty-third President of the United States.

Harrison won the presidential election of 1888.

Harrison was the first President to represent Indiana.

Harrison chaired the US Senate Committee on Transportation Routes to the Seaboard (1881-1883) and the Committee on Territories (1883-1887).

Harrison was the first President whose grandfather had served as President (William Henry Harrison).

Harrison sought reelection in 1892, but lost to Grover Cleveland.

Harrison was the first President to die in Indiana.

ELECTION OF 1888

Benjamin Harrison (Republican): 233 electoral votes, 5,443,633 popular votes (elected President)

Grover Cleveland (Democratic): 168 electoral votes, 5,538,163 popular votes

Clinton Fisk (Prohibition): 0 electoral votes, 250,017 popular votes

Alson Streeter (Union Labor): 0 electoral votes, 149,115 popular votes

Others: 0 electoral votes, 7,918 popular votes

William McKinley, Jr.

KNOWN AS: William McKinley

DATE OF BIRTH: January 29, 1843

PLACE OF BIRTH: Niles, Ohio

COLLEGE: Allegheny College, did not graduate

PROFESSION: Teacher, Lawyer

POLITICAL PARTY: Republican

STATE REPRESENTED: Ohio

OTHER SERVICE: US Army (Captain), Stark County, Ohio Prosecuting Attorney (1869-1871), US House of Representatives (1877-1884, 1885-1891), Governor of Ohio (1891-1896)

TERM AS PRESIDENT: March 4, 1897-September 14, 1901 (4 years, 194 days)

AGE AT INAUGURATION: 54 years 34 days

VICE PRESIDENTS: Garret A. Hobart (1897-1899), Theodore Roosevelt (1901)

LIVED AFTER TERM: Died in Office

DATE OF DEATH: September 14, 1901

AGE AT DEATH: 58 years, 228 days

PLACE OF DEATH: Buffalo, New York

PLACE OF BURIAL: McKinley Monument, Canton, Ohio

SOME FACTS ABOUT MCKINLEY:

McKinley was the twenty-fifth President of the United States.

McKinley won the presidential elections of 1896 and 1900.

McKinley served from November 21, 1899 to March 3, 1901 without a President due to the death of Garret Hobart.

McKinley died at the hands of an assassination. On September 6, 1901, anarchist Leon Czolgosz shot the President in Buffalo, New York. McKinley died on September 14.

McKinley chaired the US House Committee on the Revision of the Laws (1881-1883), and the Ways and Means Committee (1889-1891).

McKinley was the last President to see active service in the American Civil War.

ELECTION OF 1896

William McKinley (Republican): 271 electoral votes, 7,112,138 popular votes (elected President)

William J. Bryan (Democratic): 176 electoral votes, 6,510,807 popular votes

John Palmer (National Democratic): 0 electoral votes, 133,537 popular votes

Joshua Levering (Prohibition): 0 electoral votes, 124,896 popular votes

Others: 0 electoral votes, 57,296 popular votes

ELECTION OF 1900

William McKinley (Republican): 292 electoral votes, 7,218,283 popular votes (reelected President)

William J. Bryan (Democratic): 155 electoral votes, 6,358,149 popular votes

John Woolley (Prohibition): 0 electoral votes, 209,132 popular votes

Eugene Debs (Socialist): 0 electoral votes, 86,973 popular votes

Others: 0 electoral votes, 86,973 popular votes

Theodore Roosevelt, Jr.

KNOWN AS: Theodore Roosevelt

DATE OF BIRTH: October 28, 1858

PLACE OF BIRTH: New York, New York

COLLEGE: Harvard, graduated in 1880

PROFESSIONS: Rancher, Author, Politics

POLITICAL PARTY: Republican

STATE REPRESENTED: New York

OTHER SERVICE: US Army (Colonel), New York State Assembly (182-1884), United States Civil Service Commission (1889-1895), President of the New York Board of Police Commissioners (1895-1897), Under Secretary of the Navy (1897-1898), Governor of New York (1899-1900), Vice President (1901)

TERM AS PRESIDENT: September 14, 1901-March 3, 1909 (7 years, 171 days)

AGE AT INAUGURATION: 42 years, 322 days

VICE PRESIDENT: Charles W. Fairbanks (1905-1909)

OCCUPATION AFTER TERM: Author, Explorer, Politics

LIVED AFTER TERM: 9 years, 309 days

DATE OF DEATH: January 6, 1919

AGE AT DEATH: 60 years, 71 days

PLACE OF DEATH: Oyster Bay, New York

PLACE OF BURIAL: Youngs Memorial Cemetery, Oyster Bay, New York

SOME FACTS ABOUT ROOSEVELT:

Roosevelt was the twenty-sixth President of the United States.

Roosevelt was the twenty-fifth Vice President of the United States.

Roosevelt won the presidential election of 1904.

Roosevelt was the first President to be administered the oath of office in Buffalo, New York.

Roosevelt was the first President to win election to the office after first gaining it through the death of his predecessor.

Roosevelt served without a Vice President from September 14, 1901 to March 3, 1905.

Roosevelt was the first President to win a Nobel Peace Prize (1906).

Roosevelt was the youngest person to serve as President.

Roosevelt sought election as President on the Progressive Ticket in 1912. He lost to Woodrow Wilson.

Roosevelt survived an assassination attempt while campaigning for President on October 14, 1912. John Nepomuk Schrank shot Roosevelt in the chest.

ELECTION OF 1904

Theodore Roosevelt (Republican): 336 electoral votes, 7,630,557 popular votes (elected President)

Alton Parker (Democratic): 140 electoral votes, 5,084,537 popular votes

Eugene Debs (Socialist): 0 electoral votes, 402,810 popular votes

Silas Swallow (Prohibition): 0 electoral votes, 259,103 popular votes

Others: 0 electoral votes, 148,752 popular votes,

William Howard Taft

KNOWN AS: William H. Taft

DATE OF BIRTH: September 15, 1857

PLACE OF BIRTH: Cincinnati, Ohio

COLLEGE: Yale, graduated in 1878

PROFESSION: Lawyer

POLITICAL PARTY: Republican

STATE REPRESENTED: Ohio

OTHER SERVICE: Connecticut Home Guard (no specific rank), Assistant District Attorney, Cincinnati, Ohio (1881-1882), Assistant City Solicitor, Cincinnati (1887), Judge of the Superior Court of Cincinnati (1887-1890), US Solicitor General (1890-1892), Justice, US Circuit Court (1892-1900), President of the Philippines Commission (1900-1901), Governor-General of the Philippine Islands (1901-1904), Secretary of War (1904-1908), Provisional Governor of Cuba (1907), Chief Justice, US Supreme Court (1921-1930)

TERM AS PRESIDENT: March 4, 1909- March 3, 1913 (4 years)

AGE AT INAUGURATION: 51 years, 170 days

VICE PRESIDENT: James S. Sherman (1909-1912)

OCCUPATION AFTER TERM: Jurist, Chief Justice of the United States Supreme Court

LIVED AFTER TERM: 17 years, 4 days

DATE OF DEATH: March 8, 1930

AGE AT DEATH: 72 years, 174 days

PLACE OF DEATH: Washington, D. C.

PLACE OF BURIAL: Arlington National Cemetery, Arlington, Virginia

SOME FACTS ABOUT TAFT:

Taft was the twenty-seventh President of the United States.

Taft won the presidential election of 1908.

Taft served without a Vice President from October 30, 1912 to March 3, 1913 due to the death of James S. Sherman.

Taft was the Republican nominee for President in 1912. He finished behind Woodrow Wilson and Theodore Roosevelt.

Taft was the first Republican nominee to finish third in a presidential election.

Taft began the tradition of a President throwing out the first ball to commence the Major League baseball season.

Taft was the first former President to serve as Chief Justice of the US Supreme Court.

Taft was the first President buried at Arlington National Cemetery.

ELECTION OF 1908

William H, Taft (Republican): 321 electoral votes, 7,678,174 popular votes (elected President)

William J. Bryan (Democratic): 162 electoral votes, 6,409,007 popular votes

Eugene Debs (Socialist): 0 electoral votes, 420,856 popular votes

Eugene Chafin (Prohibition): 0 electoral votes, 254,081 popular votes

Others: 0 electoral votes, 126,991 popular votes

Thomas Woodrow Wilson

KNOWN AS: Woodrow Wilson

DATE OF BIRTH: December 19, 1856

PLACE OF BIRTH: Staunton, Virginia

COLLEGE: Princeton, graduated in 1879

PROFESSIONS: Professor, Lawyer, College President

POLITICAL PARTY: Democratic

STATE REPRESENTED: New Jersey

OTHER SERVICE: Governor of New Jersey (1911-1913)

TERM AS PRESIDENT: March 4, 1913-March 3, 1921 (8 years)

AGE AT INAUGURATION: 56 years, 65 days

VICE PRESIDENT: Thomas R. Marshall (1913-1921)

OCCUPATION AFTER TERM: Lawyer

LIVED AFTER TERM: 2 years, 337 days

DATE OF DEATH: February 3, 1924

AGE AT DEATH: 67 years, 36 days

PLACE OF DEATH: Washington, D. C.

PLACE OF BURIAL: Washington National Cathedral, Washington, D. C.

SOME FACTS ABOUT WILSON

Wilson was the twenty-eight President of the United States.

Wilson won the presidential elections of 1912 and 1916.

Wilson was the first President to represent New Jersey.

Wilson stopped using his first name, Stephen, in his youth.

ELECTION OF 1912

Woodrow Wilson (Democratic): 435 electoral votes, 6,294,284 popular votes (elected President)

Theodore Roosevelt (Progressive): 88 electoral votes, 4,120,609 popular votes

William H. Taft (Republican): 8 electoral votes, 3,487,937 popular

Eugene Debs (Socialist) 0 electoral votes, 900,742 popular votes

Others: 0 electoral votes, 241,975 popular votes

ELECTION OF 1916

Woodrow Wilson (Democratic): 277 electoral votes, 9,130,861 popular votes (reelected President)

Charles Hughes (Republican): 254 electoral votes, 8,549,700 popular votes

Allan Benson (Socialist): 0 electoral votes, 590,190 popular votes

James Hanly (Prohibition): 0 electoral votes, 221,302 popular votes

Others: 0 electoral votes, 49,265 popular votes

Warren Gamaliel Harding

KNOWN AS: Warren G. Harding

DATE OF BIRTH: November 2, 1865

PLACE OF BIRTH: Corsica, Ohio

COLLEGE: Ohio Central College, did not graduate

PROFESSION: Newspaper editor and publisher

POLITICAL PARTY: Republican

STATE REPRESENTED: Ohio

OTHER SERVICE: Ohio State Senate (1899-1903), Lieutenant Governor of Ohio (1904-1905), US Senate (1915-1921)

TERM AS PRESIDENT: March 4, 1921-August 2, 1923 (2 years, 151 days)

AGE AT INAUGURATION: 55 years, 122 days

VICE PRESIDENT: Calvin Coolidge (1921-1923)

LIVED AFTER TERM: Died in Office

DATE OF DEATH: August 2, 1923

AGE AT DEATH: 57 years, 273 days

PLACE OF DEATH: San Francisco, California

PLACE OF BURIAL: Marion Cemetery, Marion, Ohio – reinterred at the Harding Memorial Tomb, Marion, Ohio

SOME FACTS ABOUT HARDING:

Harding was the twenty-ninth President of the United States.

Harding won the presidential election of 1920.

Harding was the first President born after the end of the American Civil War.

Harding was the first President to deliver an address over the radio.

Harding chaired the US Senate Committee on the Philippines (1919-1921).

Harding was the first President to die in California.

ELECTION OF 1920

Warren G. Hardin (Republican): 404 electoral votes, 16,166,126 electoral votes (elected President)

James M. Cox (Democratic): 127 electoral votes, 9,140,256 popular votes

Eugene Debs (Socialist): 0 electoral votes, 914,191 popular votes

Parley Christiansen (Farmer-Labor): 0 electoral votes, 265,395 popular votes

Others: 0 electoral votes, 302,752 popular votes

John Calvin Coolidge, Jr.

KNOWN AS: Calvin Coolidge

DATE OF BIRTH: July 4, 1872

PLACE OF BIRTH: Plymouth, Vermont

COLLEGE: Amherst, graduated in 1895

PROFESSION: Lawyer

POLITICAL PARTY: Republican

STATE REPRESENTED: Massachusetts

OTHER SERVICE: City Council, Northampton, Massachusetts (1899), City Solicitor, Northampton, Massachusetts (1900-1901), Clerk of Courts, Hampshire County, Massachusetts (1903-1904), Massachusetts House of Representatives (1907-1908), Mayor of Northampton, Massachusetts (1910-1911), Massachusetts State Senate (1912-1915), President of the Massachusetts State Senate (1914-1915), Lieutenant Governor of Massachusetts (1916-1918), Governor of Massachusetts (1919-1920), Vice President (1921-1923)

TERM AS PRESIDENT: August 2, 1923-March 3, 1929, (5 years, 214 days)

AGE AT INAUGURATION: 51 years, 30 days

VICE PRESIDENT: Charles G. Dawes (1925-1929)

OCCUPATION AFTER TERM: Author

LIVED AFTER TERM: 3 years, 307 days

DATE OF DEATH: January 5, 1933

AGE AT DEATH: 60, 185 days

PLACE OF DEATH: Northampton, Massachusetts.

PLACE OF BURIAL: Plymouth Notch Cemetery, Plymouth, Vermont

SOME FACTS ABOUT COOLIDGE

Coolidge was the thirtieth President of the United State.

Coolidge was the twenty-ninth Vice President of the United States.

Coolidge was the first President to be administered the oath of office in Plymouth Notch, Vermont.

Coolidge won the presidential election of 1924.

Coolidge served without a Vice President from August 3, 1923 to March 4, 1925.

Coolidge was the first President to be administered the oath of office by his father (John Calvin Coolidge in 1923).

Coolidge was the first President to be administered the oath of office by a former President (William Howard Taft in 1925).

ELECTION OF 1924

Calvin Coolidge (Republican): 382 electoral votes, 15,719,068 popular votes (elected President)

John Davis (Democratic): 136 electoral votes, 8,384,341 popular votes

Robert LaFollette (Progressive): 13 electoral votes, 4,833,821 popular votes

Others: 0 electoral votes, 155,394 popular votes

Herbert Clark Hoover

KNOWN AS: Herbert Hoover

DATE OF BIRTH: August 10, 1874

PLACE OF BIRTH: West Branch, Iowa

COLLEGE: Stanford University, graduated in 1895

PROFESSION: Engineer

POLITICAL PARTY: Republican

STATE REPRESENTED: California

OTHER SERVICE: Chairman of Commission for Relief in Belgium (1915-1918), US Food Administrator (1917-1919), Chairman European Relief Council (1920), Secretary of Commerce (1921-1928), Coal Administration (1922), Coordinator of European Food Program (1946), Chairman of Commission on Organization of the Executive Branch of the Government (1947-1949, 1953-1955)

TERM AS PRESIDENT: March 4, 1929- March 4, 1933 (4 years)

AGE AT INAUGURATION: 54 years, 206 days

VICE PRESIDENT: Charles Curtis (1929-1933)

OCCUPATION AFTER TERM: Government service, Author

LIVED AFTER TERM: 31 years, 231 days

DATE OF DEATH: October 20, 1964

AGE AT DEATH: 90 years, 71 days

PLACE OF DEATH: New York, New York

PLACE OF BURIAL: Herbert Hoover National Historic Site, West Branch, Iowa

SOME FACTS ABOUT HOOVER

Hoover was the thirty-first President of the United States.

Hoover won the election of 1928.

Before running for President in 1928, Hoover had never sought elective office.

Hoover was the first President born west of the Mississippi.

Hoover was the first President born in Iowa.

Hoover was the first President to represent California.

Hoover was the first President to serve in a Cabinet post other than Secretary of State or Secretary of War.

Hoover was the first President to decline his presidential salary.

Hoover lost his bid for reelection to Franklin D. Roosevelt in 1932.

ELECTION OF 1928

Herbert Hoover (Republican): 444 electoral votes, 21,428,584 popular votes (elected President)

Alfred E. Smith (Democratic): 87 electoral votes, 15,015,863 popular votes

Norman Thomas (Socialist): 0 electoral votes, 267,519 popular votes

Others: 0 electoral votes, 96,995 popular votes

Franklin Delano Roosevelt

KNOWN AS: Franklin D. Roosevelt

DATE OF BIRTH: January 30, 1882

PLACE OF BIRTH: Hyde Park, New York

COLLEGE: Harvard, graduated in 1903

PROFESSIONS: Lawyer

POLITICAL PARTY: Democratic

STATE REPRESENTED: New York

OTHER SERVICE: New York State Senate (1911-1913), Under Secretary of the Navy (1913-1920), Governor of New York (1929-1933)

TERM AS PRESIDENT: March 4, 1933-April 12, 1945 (12 years 39 days)

AGE AT INAUGURATION: 51 years, 33 days

VICE PRESIDENTS: John Nance Garner (1933-1941), Henry A. Wallace (1941-1945), Harry S. Truman (1945)

LIVED AFTER TERM: Died in Office

DATE OF DEATH: April 12, 1945

AGE AT DEATH: 63 years, 72 days

PLACE OF DEATH: Warm Springs, Georgia

PLACE OF BURIAL: Roosevelt Home, Hyde Park, New York

SOME FACTS ABOUT ROOSEVELT

Roosevelt was the thirty-second President of the United States.

Roosevelt won the elections of 1932, 1936, 1940, and 1944.

Roosevelt was the Democratic nominee for Vice President in 1920 on the unsuccessful ticket headed by James M. Cox.

Roosevelt contracted polio in 1921. He spent the rest of his life confined to a wheelchair.

Roosevelt served as President longer than any other person has.

Roosevelt is the only person elected President more than twice. He won election to the presidency four times.

Roosevelt is the only person to receive a majority of the popular vote in more than two presidential elections. He received a majority four times.

Roosevelt was the first President to be part of four successful national tickets.

Roosevelt is the only President to have more than two Vice Presidents. He had three.

Roosevelt appointed nine Justices to the Supreme Court.

Roosevelt was the first President to die in Georgia.

ELECTION OF 1932

Franklin D. Roosevelt (Democratic): 472 electoral votes, 22,821,513 popular votes (elected President)

Herbert Hoover (Republican): 59 electoral votes, 15,761,532 popular votes

Norman Thomas (Socialist): 0 electoral votes, 884,895 popular votes

William Foster (Communist): 0 electoral votes, 103,314 popular votes

Others: 0 electoral votes, 181,200 popular votes

ELECTION OF 1936

Franklin D. Roosevelt (Democratic): 523 electoral votes, 27,757,431 popular votes (reelected President)

Alfred Landon (Republican): 8 electoral votes, 16,683,574 popular votes

William Lemke (Union): 0 electoral votes, 892,381 popular votes

Norman Thomas (Socialist): 0 electoral votes, 187,971 popular votes

Others: 0 electoral votes, 133,031 popular votes

ELECTION OF 1940

Franklin D. Roosevelt (Democratic): 449 electoral votes, 27,314,449 popular votes (reelected President)

Wendell Willkie (Republican): 82 electoral votes, 22,348,343 popular votes

Others: 0 electoral votes, 250,060 popular votes

ELECTION OF 1944

Franklin D. Roosevelt (Democratic): 432 electoral votes, 25,612,916 popular votes (reelected President)

Thomas E. Dewey (Republican): 99 electoral votes, 22,017,929 popular votes

Others: 0 electoral votes, 346,247 popular votes

Harry S. Truman

DATE OF BIRTH: May 8, 1884

PLACE OF BIRTH: Lamar, Missouri

COLLEGE: None

PROFESSIONS: Farmer, Clothing Dealer

POLITICAL PARTY: Democratic

STATE REPRESENTED: Missouri

OTHER SERVICE: US Army (Colonel) Judge of Jackson County (Missouri) Court (1922-1924), Presiding Judge, Jackson County Court (1926-1934), US Senate (1935-1945), Vice President (1945)

TERM AS PRESIDENT: April 12, 1945- January 20, 1953 (7 years, 283 days)

AGE AT INAUGURATION: 60 years 339 days

VICE PRESIDENT: Alben W. Barkley (1949-1953)

OCCUPATION AFTER TERM: Author

LIVED AFTER TERM: 19 years, 340 days

DATE OF DEATH: December 26, 1972

AGE AT DEATH: 88 years, 232 days

PLACE OF DEATH: Independence, Missouri

PLACE OF BURIAL: Truman Presidential Library and Museum, Independence, Missouri

SOME FACTS ABOUT TRUMAN

Truman was the thirty-third President of the United States.

Truman was the thirty-fourth Vice President of the United States.

Truman won the presidential election of 1948.

Truman served without a Vice President from April 12, 1945 to January 20, 1949.

Truman was the first President born in Missouri.

Truman was the first President to represent Missouri.

Truman was the last President not to earn a college degree.

Truman's middle initial did not stand for anything.

Truman chaired the US Senate Special Committee to Investigate the National Defense Program (1941-1944).

Truman was the first President to appear on television.

Truman survived an assassination attempt on November 1, 1950. Two Puerto Rican nationalists attempted to shoot their way into the Blair House. They never got to the President. Truman was residing at the Blair House while due to ongoing renovations at the White House.

Truman was the first President to die in Missouri.

ELECTION OF 1948

Harry S. Truman (Democratic): 303 electoral votes, 24,179,347 popular votes (elected President)

Thomas E. Dewey (Republican): 189 electoral votes, 21,991,292 popular votes

J. Strom Thurmond (National States Rights Democratic): 39 electoral votes, 1,175,946 popular votes

Henry A. Wallace (Progressive): 0 electoral votes, 1,157,328 popular votes

Others: 0 electoral votes, 290,797 popular votes

Dwight David Eisenhower

KNOWN AS: Dwight D. Eisenhower

DATE OF BIRTH: October 14, 1890

PLACE OF BIRTH: Denison, Texas

COLLEGE: United States Military Academy, at West Point, New York, graduated in 1915

PROFESSION: Military

POLITICAL PARTY: Republican

STATE REPRESENTED: New York

OTHER SERVICE: US Army (General of the Army)

TERM AS PRESIDENT: January 20, 1953-January 20, 1961 (8 years)

AGE AT INAUGURATION: 62 years, 98 days

VICE PRESIDENT: Richard M. Nixon (1953-1961)

OCCUPATION AFTER TERM: Author

LIVED AFTER TERM: 8 years, 67 days

DATE OF DEATH: March 28, 1969

AGE AT DEATH: 78 years, 165 days

PLACE OF DEATH: Washington D. C.

PLACE OF BURIAL: Eisenhower Center, Abilene, Kansas

SOME FACTS ABOUT EISENHOWER

Eisenhower was the thirty-fourth President of the United States.

Eisenhower won the 1952 and 1956 presidential elections.

Eisenhower's given name was David Dwight Eisenhower, but he switched his first two names and went by Dwight David Eisenhower.

Eisenhower never sought any political office before running for President.

Eisenhower held the highest rank possible in the US Army. He was a Five-Star General.

Eisenhower was the first President legally barred from seeking a third term due to the provisions of the 22nd Amendment.

Eisenhower was the first President born in Texas.

ELECTION OF 1952

Dwight D. Eisenhower (Republican): 442 electoral votes, 34,075,529 popular votes (elected President)

Adlai Stevenson (Democratic): 89 electoral votes, 27,375,090 popular votes

Others: 0 electoral votes, 301,323 popular votes

ELECTION OF 1956

Dwight D. Eisenhower (Republican): 457 electoral votes, 35,579,180 popular votes (reelected President)

Adlai Stevenson (Democratic): 73 electoral votes, 26,028,028 popular votes

Others: 1 electoral vote, 414,711 popular votes (See note below)

Note: 1 elector from Alabama pledged to Stevenson voted for Walter Jones.

John Fitzgerald Kennedy

KNOWN AS: John F. Kennedy

DATE OF BIRTH: May 29, 1917

PLACE OF BIRTH: Brookline, Massachusetts

COLLEGE: Harvard, graduated in 1940

PROFESSION: Author, Politics

POLITICAL PARTY: Democratic

STATE REPRESENTED: Massachusetts

OTHER SERVICE: US Navy (Lieutenant), US House of Representatives (1947-1953), US Senate (1953-1960)

TERM AS PRESIDENT: January 20, 1961-November 22, 1963 (2 years, 206 days)

AGE AT INAUGURATION: 43 years, 236 days

VICE PRESIDENT: Lyndon B. Johnson (1961-1963)

LIVED AFTER TERM: Died in Office

DATE OF DEATH: November 22, 1963

AGE AT DEATH: 46 years, 177 days

PLACE OF DEATH: Dallas, Texas

PLACE OF BURIAL: Arlington National Cemetery, Arlington, Virginia

SOME FACTS ABOUT KENNEDY

Kennedy was the thirty-fifth President of the United States.

Kennedy won the 1960 election.

Kennedy was the first President born in the Twentieth Century.

Kennedy was the first President who was a member of the Roman Catholic Church.

Kennedy was the first President who had served in the US Navy.

Kennedy was the youngest person ever elected President.

Kennedy won a Pulitzer Prize in 1957 for his book, *Profiles in Courage.*

Kennedy chaired the US Senate Special Committee on the Senate Reception Room (1957-1960).

Kennedy was the first President to die in Texas.

Kennedy died at the hands of an assassination. A sniper shot and killed Kennedy on November 22, 1963 in Dallas, Texas. Authorities arrested Lee Harvey Oswald for the crime, but Jack Ruby murdered Oswald before the suspected assassin went to trial.

ELECTION OF 1960

John F. Kennedy (Democratic): 303 electoral votes, 34,220,984 popular votes (elected President)

Richard M. Nixon (Republican): 219 electoral votes, 34,108,157 popular votes

Harry F. Byrd (independent): 15 electoral votes, 0 popular votes (See note below)

Others: 0 electoral votes, 503,342 popular votes

Note: Byrd received the votes of 8 "unpledged electors" from Mississippi, 6 "free electors" from Alabama, and 1 elector pledged to Nixon from Oklahoma.

Lyndon Baines Johnson

KNOWN AS: Lyndon B. Johnson

DATE OF BIRTH: August 27, 1908

PLACE OF BIRTH: Near Stonewall, Texas

COLLEGE: Southwest Texas State College (now Texas State University), graduated in 1930

PROFESSION: Rancher, Teacher

POLITICAL PARTY: Democratic

STATE REPRESENTED: Texas

OTHER SERVICE: US Navy (Lieutenant Commander), Director of the National Youth Association of Texas (1935-1937), US House of Representatives (1937-1949), US Senate (1949-1961), Senate Majority Leader (1955-1961), Vice President (1961-1963)

TERM AS PRESIDENT: 5 years, 59 days

AGE AT INAUGURATION: 55 years, 87 days

VICE PRESIDENT: Hubert H. Humphrey (1965-1969)

OCCUPATION AFTER TERM: Rancher, Author

LIVED AFTER TERM: 4 years, 2 days

DATE OF DEATH: January 22, 1973

AGE AT DEATH: 64 years, 148 days

PLACE OF DEATH: San Antonio, Texas

PLACE OF BURIAL: LBJ Ranch, Stonewall (Johnson City), Texas

SOME FACTS ABOUT JOHNSON

Johnson was the thirty-sixth President of the United State.

Johnson was the thirty-seventh Vice President of the United States.

Johnson was the first President to be administered the oath of office in Dallas, Texas

Johnson won the presidential election of 1964.

Johnson was the first President to represent Texas.

Johnson was the first resident of a southern state to win a presidential election since Zachary Taylor in 1848.

Johnson was the first resident of a southern state to serve as President since Andrew Johnson (1861-1865).

Johnson was the first Democrat to carry Vermont in a presidential election.

Johnson was the first member of Congress to enlist in the military at the outbreak of World War II.

Johnson was the first President who had served as a Whip in the US Senate.

Johnson was the first President who had served as Senate Minority Leader.

Johnson was the first President who had served as Senate Majority Leader.

Johnson chaired the US Senate Special Committee on the Senate Reception Room (1955-1956), the Special Committee on Astronautics and Space (1957-1958), and the Committee on Aeronautical and Space Sciences (1957-1960).

ELECTION OF 1964

Lyndon B. Johnson (Democratic): 486 electoral votes, 43,129,040 popular votes (elected President)

Barry Goldwater: 52 electoral votes, 27,175,754 popular votes

Others: 0 electoral votes, 336,735 popular votes

Richard Milhous Nixon

KNOWN AS: Richard M. Nixon

DATE OF BIRTH: January 9, 1913

PLACE OF BIRTH: Yorba Linda, California

COLLEGE: Whittier College, graduated in 1934

PROFESSION: Lawyer

POLITICAL PARTY: Republican

STATE REPRESENTED: New York

OTHER SERVICE: US Navy (Lieutenant Commander), US House of Representatives (1947-1950), US Senate (1950-1953), Vice President (1953-1961)

TERM AS PRESIDENT: January 20, 1969-August 9, 1974, 5 years, 201 days

AGE AT INAUGURATION: 56 years, 11 days

VICE PRESIDENTS: Spiro Agnew (1969-1973), Gerald R. Ford (1973-1974)

OCCUPATION AFTER TERM: Author

LIVED AFTER TERM: 19 years, 257 days

DATE OF DEATH: April 22, 1994

AGE AT DEATH: 81 years, 103 days

PLACE OF DEATH: New York, New York

PLACE OF BURIAL: Richard Nixon Library and Birthplace, Yorba Linda, California

SOME FACTS ABOUT NIXON

Nixon was the thirty-seventh President of the United States.

Nixon was the thirty-sixth Vice President of the United States.

Nixon won the presidential elections of 1968 and 1972.

Nixon is the only President to resign from office.

Nixon was the Republican nominee for President in 1960. He lost to John Kennedy.

Nixon was the first member of the Republican Party to serve eight consecutive years as Vice President.

Nixon is the only person to win election as President and Vice President twice each.

Nixon was the first President born in California.

Nixon was the first presidential candidate to carry forty-nine states.

Nixon was the first President to accept a presidential pardon to avoid possible criminal prosecution.

Nixon served without a Vice President from October 19, 1973 to December 6, 1973 due to the resignation of Spiro T. Agnew.

Nixon was the first sitting President to visit The People's Republic of China.

ELECTION OF 1968

Richard Nixon (Republican): 301 electoral votes, 31,783,783 popular votes (elected President)

Hubert Humphrey (Democratic): 191 electoral votes, 31,271,839 popular votes

George Wallace (American Independent): 46 electoral votes, 9,901,118 popular votes (See note below)

Others: 0 electoral votes, 243,259

Note: 1 elector from Tennessee pledged to Nixon voted for Wallace.

ELECTION OF 1972

Richard Nixon (Republican): 520 electoral votes, 47,168,710 popular votes (reelected President)

George McGovern (Democratic): 17 electoral votes, 29,173,222 popular votes

John Hospers (Libertarian): 1 electoral vote, 3,674 popular votes (See note below)

John Schmitz (American Independent): 0 electoral votes, 1,100,896 popular votes

Others: 0 electoral votes, 297,528 popular votes

Note: 1 elector from Virginia pledged to Nixon voted for John Hospers.

Gerald Rudolph. Ford, Jr.

KNOWN AS: Gerald R. Ford

DATE OF BIRTH: July 14, 1913

PLACE OF BIRTH: Omaha, Nebraska

COLLEGE: University of Michigan, graduated in 1935

PROFESSION: Lawyer

POLITICAL PARTY: Republican

STATE REPRESENTED: Michigan

OTHER SERVICE: US Navy (Lieutenant Commander), US House of Representatives (1949-1973), House Minority Leader (1965-1973)

TERM AS PRESIDENT: August 9, 1974-January 20, 1977 (2 years, 164 days)

AGE AT INAUGURATION: 61 years, 26 days

VICE PRESIDENT: Nelson Rockefeller (1974-1977)

OCCUPATION AFTER TERM: Author, Retired

LIVED AFTER TERM: 29 years, 340 days

DATE OF DEATH: December 26, 2006

AGE AT DEATH: 93 years, 165 days

PLACE OF DEATH: Rancho Mirage, Californian

PLACE OF BURIAL: Gerald R. Ford Museum, Grand Rapids, Michigan

SOME FACTS ABOUT FORD

Ford was the thirty-eighth President of the United States.

Ford was the fortieth Vice President of the United States.

Ford was the first Vice President to assume office under the provisions of the twenty-fifth Amendment.

Ford was the first President to assume office under the provisions of the twenty-fifth Amendment.

Ford was unsuccessful in his bid for election to the presidency in 1976.

Ford served without a Vice President from August 9, 1974 to December 19, 1974.

Ford was the first President who had served as House Minority Leader.

Ford was the first President born in Nebraska.

Ford was the first President to represent Michigan.

Ford was the first sitting President to visit Japan.

Ford never won a presidential election.

Ford was an All-American football player at the University of Michigan.

Ford survived two assassination attempts in September 1975. On September 5, a follower of Charles Manson, Lynette "Squeaky" Fromme, attempted to shoot Ford, but her pistol was on "safe" and did not fire. On September 22, Sara

Jane Moore fired two rounds from her pistol at Ford, but missed the President.

Ford's original name was Leslie Lynch King, Jr. Ford's adoptive father gave him the name Gerald Rudolph Ford, Jr.

James Earl Carter, Jr.

KNOWN AS: Jimmy Carter

DATE OF BIRTH: October 1, 1924

PLACE OF BIRTH: Plains, Georgia

COLLEGE: US Naval Academy, graduated in 1946

PROFESSIONS: Sailor, Peanut business

POLITICAL PARTY: Democratic

STATE REPRESENTED: Georgia

OTHER SERVICE: US Navy (Lieutenant Commander), Chairman of the Sumter County, Georgia Board of Education (1955-1962), Georgia State Senate (1963-1966), Governor of Georgia (1971-1975), Democratic National Campaign Committee Chair (1974)

TERM AS PRESIDENT: January 20, 1977-January 20, 1981 (4 years)

AGE AT INAUGURATION: 52 years, 111 days

VICE PRESIDENT: Walter Mondale (1977-1981)

OCCUPATION AFTER TERM: Author, Lecturer, Philanthropy

SOME FACTS ABOUT CARTER

Carter was the thirty-ninth President of the United States.

Carter won the 1976 presidential election.

Carter preferred persons call him by his nickname "Jimmy".

Carter was the first President sworn into office using his nickname.

Carter was the unsuccessful Democratic nominee for President in 1980.

Carter was the first President born in Georgia.

Carter was the first President to represent Georgia.

Carter was the first President born in a hospital.

ELECTION OF 1976

Jimmy Carter (Democratic): 297 electoral votes, 40,831,881 popular votes (elected President)

Gerald Ford (Republican): 240 electoral votes, 39,148,634 popular votes

Eugene McCarthy (independent): 0 electoral votes, 744,763 popular votes

Others: 1 electoral vote, 815,502 popular votes (See note below)

Note: 1 elector from Washington pledged to Ford voted for Ronald Reagan.

Ronald Wilson Reagan

KNOWN AS: Ronald Wilson

DATE OF BIRTH: February 6, 1911

PLACE OF BIRTH: Tampico, Illinois

COLLEGE: Eureka College, graduated in 1932

PROFESSION: Actor, Lecturer

POLITICAL PARTY: Republican

STATE REPRESENTED: California

OTHER SERVICE: US Army (Captain), California Governor (1967-1975)

TERM AS PRESIDENT: January 20, 1981-January 20, 1989 (8 years)

AGE AT INAUGURATION: 69 years, 349 days

VICE PRESIDENT: George H. W. Bush (1981-1989)

OCCUPATION AFTER TERM: Author, retired

LIVED AFTER TERM: 15 years, 137 days

DATE OF DEATH: June 5, 2004

AGE AT DEATH: 93 years, 120 days

PLACE OF DEATH: Bel Air, California

PLACE OF BURIAL: Ronald Reagan Presidential Library, Simi Valley, California

SOME FACTS ABOUT REAGAN

Reagan was the fortieth President of the United States.

Reagan won the 1980 and the 1984 presidential elections.

Reagan was the first President born in Illinois.

Reagan was the first President who had served as a union President. He led the Screen Actors Guild (1947-1960).

Reagan was the first President who had hosted a weekly television show.

Reagan was the first President to survive wounds received by a would-be assassin. On March 30, 1981, John Hinckley, Jr. shot Reagan and several others in Washington, D. C. After several weeks spent recuperating, Reagan returned to work.

Reagan was the first President to appoint a woman to the US Supreme Court.

Reagan unsuccessfully sought the Republican presidential nomination in 1968 and 1976.

Reagan received one electoral vote pledged to Gerald Ford in 1976.

ELECTION OF 1980

Ronald Reagan (Republican): 489 electoral votes, 43,903,230 popular votes (elected President)

Jimmy Carter (Democratic): 49 electoral votes, 35,480,115 popular votes

John Anderson (independent): 0 electoral votes, 5,719,850 popular votes

Edward Clark (Libertarian): 0 electoral votes, 921,128 popular votes

Others: 0 electoral votes, 485,355 popular votes

ELECTION OF 1984

Ronald Reagan (Republican): 525 electoral votes, 54,455,472 popular votes (reelected President)

Walter Mondale (Democratic): 13 electoral votes, 37,577,352

Others: 0 electoral votes, 620,409 popular votes

George Herbert Walker Bush

KNOWN AS: George Bush

DATE OF BIRTH: June 12, 1924

PLACE OF BIRTH: Milton, Massachusetts

COLLEGE: Yale, graduated in 1948

PROFESSION: Oil business

POLITICAL PARTY: Republican

STATE REPRESENTED: Texas

OTHER SERVICE: US Navy (Lieutenant, Junior Grade), US House of Representatives (1967-1971), Ambassador to the United Nations (1971-1973), Republican National Committee chair (1973-1974), US liaison officer (with the rank of Ambassador) to the People's Republic of China (1974-1976), CIA Director (1976-1977), Vice President (1981-1989)

TERM AS PRESIDENT: January 20, 1989-January 20, 1993 (4 years)

AGE AT INAUGURATION: 64 years, 233 days

VICE PRESIDENT: James Danforth (Dan) Quayle (1989-1993)

OCCUPATION AFTER TERM: Philanthropy

SOME FACTS ABOUT BUSH

Bush was the forty-first President of the United States.

Bush was the forty-third Vice President of the United States.

Bush won the presidential election of 1988.

Bush was the unsuccessful Republican nominee for reelection in 1992.

Bush's son, George Walker Bush also served as America's Chief Executive.

Bush was the first President who had served as the Director of Central Intelligence Agency.

ELECTION OF 1988

George H. W. Bush (Republican): 426 electoral votes, 48,886,597 popular votes (elected President)

Michael Dukakis (Democratic): 111 electoral votes, 41,809,476 popular votes

Ron Paul (Libertarian): 0 electoral votes, 431,750 popular votes

Others: 1 electoral vote, 466,863 popular votes (See note below)

Note: 1 elector from West Virginia pledged to Dukakis voted for Lloyd Bensten.

William Jefferson Clinton

KNOWN AS: Bill Clinton

DATE OF BIRTH: August 14, 1946

PLACE OF BIRTH: Hope, Arkansas

COLLEGE: Georgetown University (Washington, D. C.), graduated in 1968

PROFESSION: Lawyer

POLITICAL PARTY: Democratic

STATE REPRESENTED: Arkansas

OTHER SERVICE: Arkansas Attorney General (1977-1979), Arkansas Governor (1979-1981, 1983-1992)

TERM AS PRESIDENT: January 20, 1993-January 20, 2001 (8 years)

AGE AT INAUGURATION: 46 years, 159 days

VICE PRESIDENT: Albert Gore, Jr. (1993-2001)

OCCUPATION AFTER TERM: Politics, Philanthropy

SOME FACTS ABOUT CLINTON

Clinton was the forty-second President of the United States.

Clinton won the presidential elections of 1992 and 1996.

Clinton was the first President born in Arkansas.

Clinton was the first President to represent Arkansas.

Clinton was the first President born after the end of World War II.

The US House of Representatives impeached Clinton (1998). The US Senate acquitted him (1999).

Clinton was the first President disbarred from the practice of law.

Clinton was the first former President whose spouse was the presidential nominee of a major party – Hillary Clinton in 2016.

Clinton's original name was William Jefferson Blythe, Jr. Clinton took his last name from his adoptive father.

ELECTION OF 1992

Bill Clinton (Democratic): 370 electoral votes, 44,909,806 popular votes (elected President)

George Bush (Republican): 168 electoral votes, 39,104,550 popular votes

H. Ross Perot (independent): 0 electoral votes, 19,743,821 popular votes

Andre Marrou (Libertarian): 0 electoral votes, 290,087 popular votes

Others: 0 electoral votes, 378,347 popular votes

ELECTION OF 1996

Bill Clinton (Democratic): 379 electoral votes, 47,400,125 popular votes (reelected President)

Robert (Bob) Dole (Republican): 159 electoral votes, 39,198,755 popular votes

H. Ross Perot (Reform): 0 electoral votes, 8,085,402 popular votes

Ralph Nader (Green): 0 electoral votes, 685,435 popular votes

Others: 0 electoral votes, 905,923 popular votes

George Walker Bush

KNOWN AS: George W. Bush

DATE OF BIRTH: July 6, 1946

PLACE OF BIRTH: New Haven, Connecticut

COLLEGE: Yale, graduated in 1968

PROFESSION: Business Executive

POLITICAL PARTY: Republican

STATE REPRESENTED: Texas

OTHER SERVICE: Texas Air National Guard (1st Lieutenant), Texas Governor (1995-2001)

TERM AS PRESIDENT: January 20, 2001-January 20, 2009 (8 years)

AGE AT INAUGURATION: 54 years, 198 days

VICE PRESIDENT: Richard "Dick" Cheney (2001-2009)

OCCUPATION AFTER TERM: Author, Philanthropy

SOME FACTS ABOUT BUSH

Bush was the forty-third President of the United States.

Bush won the presidential elections of 2000 and 2004.

Bush was the first President born in Connecticut.

Bush was the first Republican to carry Georgia twice.

Bush survived an assassination attempt in 2005. On May 10, 2005 while Bush was visiting Tilibisi, Republic of Georgia, a man threw a hand grenade at the President. The grenade did not explode.

Bush was the only President to have earned a Masters of Business Administration (M. B. A.) degree.

Bush owned the Texas Rangers baseball team from 1989 to 1994.

ELECTION OF 2000

George W. Bush (Republican): 271 electoral votes, 50,462,412 popular votes (elected President)

Albert Gore, Jr. (Democratic): 266 electoral votes, 51,009,810 popular votes (See note below)

Ralph Nader (Green): 0 electoral votes, 2,883,443 popular votes

Patrick Buchanan (Reform): 0 electoral votes, 449,181 popular votes

Others: 0 electoral votes, 621,139 popular votes

Note: 1 elector from Washington D. C. pledged to Gore abstained from voting.

ELECTION OF 2004

George W. Bush (Republican): 286 electoral votes, 62,039,572 popular votes (reelected President)

John Kerry (Democratic): 251 electoral votes, 59,027,115 popular votes

Ralph Nader (independent): 0 electoral votes, 465,642 popular votes

Michael Badnarik (Libertarian): 0 electoral votes, 397,265 popular votes

Others: 1 electoral vote, 771,261 popular votes (See note below)

Note: 1 elector from Minnesota pledged to Kerry voted for John Edwards.

Barack Hussein Obama II

KNOWN AS: Barack Obama

DATE OF BIRTH: August 4, 1961

PLACE OF BIRTH: Honolulu, Hawaii

COLLEGE: Columbia University, graduated in 1983

PROFESSION: Lecturer, Lawyer

POLITICAL PARTY: Democratic

STATE REPRESENTED: Illinois

OTHER SERVICE: Illinois State Senate (1997-2004), US Senate (2005-2008)

TERM AS PRESIDENT: January 20, 2009-January 20, 2017 (8 years)

AGE AT INAUGURATION: 47 years, 150 days

VICE PRESIDENT: Joseph Biden (2009-2017)

SOME FACTS ABOUT OBAMA

Obama was the forty-fourth President of the United States.

Obama won the presidential elections in 2008 and 2012.

Obama was the first President born outside the continuous forty-eight states.

Obama was the first President born in Hawaii.

Obama was the first President of African descent.

ELECTION OF 2008

Barack Obama (Democratic): 365 electoral votes, 69,499,428 popular votes (elected President)

John McCain (Republican): 173 electoral votes, 59,950,323 popular votes

Ralph Nader (independent): 0 electoral votes, 739,278 popular votes

Bob Barr (Libertarian): 0 electoral votes, 523,433 popular votes

Others: 0 electoral votes, 761,243 popular votes

ELECTION OF 2012

Barack Obama (Democratic): 332 electoral votes, 65,918,507 popular votes (reelected President)

Mitt Romney (Republican): 206 electoral votes, 60,934,407 popular votes

Gary Johnson (Libertarian): 0 electoral votes, 1,275,923 popular votes

Jill Stein (Green): 0 electoral votes, 469,015 popular votes

Others: 0 electoral votes, 1,108,805

Donald John Trump

KNOWN AS: Donald Trump

DATE OF BIRTH: June 14, 1946

PLACE OF BIRTH: Queens, New York

COLLEGE: University of Pennsylvania (Wharton School), graduated in 1968

PROFESSION: Business, Television star

POLITICAL PARTY: Republican

STATE REPRESENTED: New York

TERM AS PRESIDENT: January 20, 2017- Present

AGE AT INAUGURATION: 72 years, 220 days

VICE PRESIDENT: Michael Pence (2017-Present)

SOME FACTS ABOUT TRUMP

Trump is the forty-fifth President of the United States.

Trump won the 2016 presidential election.

Trump was the oldest person ever elected to a first term as President.

Trump hosted a weekly television show.

ELECTION OF 2016

Donald Trump (Republican): 304 electoral votes, 62,985,106 popular votes (elected President)

Hillary Clinton (Democratic): 227 electoral votes, 65,853,625 popular votes

Gary Johnson (Libertarian): 0 electoral votes, 4,489, 233 popular votes

Jill Stein (Green): 0 electoral votes, 1,457,222 popular votes

Others: 7 electoral votes, 2,343,415 popular votes (See note below)

Note: 3 electors from Washington pledged to Clinton voted for Colin Powell and 1 elector from Washington pledged to Clinton voted for Faith Spotted Eagle. 1 elector from Hawaii pledged to Clinton voted for Bernie Sanders. 1 elector from Texas pledged to Trump voted for John Kasich and 1 elector from Texas pledged to Trump voted for Ron Paul.

Comparative Data

In this chapter, the author provides several lists comparing the Presidents with one another. The comparative data presented here is only a fraction of what the author could have included. However, due to space constraints, he had to leave many items out.

Month of Birth

The list below arranges the Presidents by month of birth.

January (4): Fillmore, McKinley, Franklin D. Roosevelt, Nixon,

February (4): Washington, William H. Harrison, Lincoln, Reagan

March (4): Madison, Jackson, Tyler, Cleveland

April (4): Jefferson, Monroe, Buchanan, Grant

May (2): Truman, Kennedy

June (2): George H. W. Bush, Trump

July (4): John Quincy Adams, Coolidge, Ford, George W. Bush

August (5): Benjamin Harrison, Hoover, Lyndon B. Johnson, Clinton, Obama

September (1): Taft

October (6): John Adams, Hays, Arthur, Theodore Roosevelt, Eisenhower, Carter

November (5): Polk, Taylor, Pierce, Garfield, Harding

December (3): Van Buren, Andrew Johnson, Wilson

Birth States

The list below arranges the Presidents by state of birth.

Virginia (8): Washington, Jefferson, Madison, Monroe, William H. Harrison, Tyler, Taylor, Wilson

Ohio (7): Grant, Hayes, Garfield, Benjamin Harrison, McKinley, Taft, Harding

New York (5): Van Buren, Fillmore, Theodore Roosevelt, Franklin D. Roosevelt, Trump

Massachusetts (4): John Adams, John Quincy Adams, Kennedy, George H. W. Bush

North Carolina (2): Polk, Andrew Johnson

Texas (2): Eisenhower, Lyndon B. Johnson

Vermont (2): Arthur, Coolidge

Arkansas (1): Clinton

California (1): Nixon

Connecticut (1): George W. Bush

Georgia (1): Carter

Hawaii (1): Obama

Illinois (1): Reagan

Iowa (1): Hoover

Kentucky (1): Lincoln

Missouri (1): Truman

Nebraska (1): Ford

New Hampshire (1): Pierce

New Jersey (1): Cleveland

Pennsylvania (1): Buchanan

South Carolina (1): Jackson

States Represented

The list below arranges the Presidents by state of residence at the time of they assumed office.

New York (9): Van Buren, Fillmore, Arthur, Cleveland, Theodore Roosevelt, Franklin D. Roosevelt, Eisenhower, Nixon, Trump

Ohio (6): William H. Harrison, Hayes, Garfield, McKinley, Taft, Harding

Virginia (5): Washington, Jefferson, Madison, Monroe, Tyler

Massachusetts (4): John Adams, John Quincy Adams, Coolidge, Kennedy

Illinois (3): Lincoln, Grant, Obama

Tennessee (3): Jackson, Polk, Andrew Johnson

Texas (3): Lyndon B. Johnson, George H. W. Bush, George W. Bush

California (2): Hoover, Reagan

Arkansas (1): Clinton

Georgia (1): Carter

Indiana (1): Benjamin Harrison

Louisiana (1): Taylor

Michigan (1): Ford

Missouri (1): Truman

New Hampshire (1): Pierce

New Jersey (1): Wilson

Pennsylvania (1): Buchanan

Relocated Presidents

Twenty American Presidents represented a state other than their birth state when they assumed office. The list below includes the names of the twenty, their birth states, and the states they represented.

Andrew Jackson: South Carolina, Tennessee

William H. Harrison: Virginia, Ohio

James K. Polk: North Carolina, Tennessee

Zachary Taylor: Virginia, Louisiana

Abraham Lincoln: Kentucky, Louisiana

Andrew Johnson: North Carolina, Tennessee

Ulysses S Grant: Ohio, Illinois

Chester A. Arthur: Vermont, New York

Grover Cleveland: New Jersey, New York

Benjamin Harrison: Ohio, Indiana

Woodrow Wilson: Virginia, New Jersey

Calvin Coolidge: Vermont, Massachusetts

Herbert Hoover: Iowa, California

Dwight D. Eisenhower: Texas, New York

Richard Nixon: California, New York

Gerald R. Ford: Nebraska, Michigan

Ronald Reagan: Illinois, California

George H. W. Bush: Massachusetts, Texas

George W. Bush: Connecticut, Texas

Barack Obama: Hawaii, Illinois

States of Death

Many Presidents relocated after their terms ended and some died at their new homes. Others died in transit or on business trips. Still others died while in Washington, D. C. The list below organizes the Presidents by the state (including Washington, D. C.) in which they died.

New York (9): Monroe, Van Buren, Fillmore, Grant, Arthur, McKinley, Theodore Roosevelt, Hoover, Nixon

Washington, D. C. (7): John Quincy Adams, William H. Harrison, Taylor, Lincoln, Taft, Wilson, Eisenhower

Virginia (4): Washington, Jefferson, Madison, Tyler

California (3): Harding, Ford, Reagan

Tennessee (3): Jackson, Polk, Andrew Johnson

Massachusetts (2): John Adams, Coolidge

New Jersey (2): Garfield, Cleveland

Texas (2): Kennedy, Lyndon B. Johnson

Georgia (1): Franklin D. Roosevelt

Indiana (1): Benjamin Harrison

Missouri (1): Truman

New Hampshire (1): Pierce

Ohio (1): Hayes

Pennsylvania (1): Buchanan

States of Burial

The list below organizes the Presidents by the state (including Washington, D. C.) of their final resting places.

Virginia (7): Washington, Jefferson, Madison, Monroe, Tyler, Taft, Kennedy

New York (6): Van Buren, Fillmore, Grant, Arthur, Theodore Roosevelt, Franklin D. Roosevelt

Ohio (5): William H. Harrison, Hayes, Garfield, McKinley, Harding

Tennessee (3): Jackson, Polk, Andrew Johnson

California (2): Nixon, Reagan

Massachusetts (2): John Adams, John Quincy Adams

Illinois (1): Lincoln

Indiana (1): Benjamin Harrison

Iowa (1): Hoover

Kansas (1): Eisenhower

Kentucky (1): Taylor

Michigan (1): Ford

Missouri (1): Truman

New Hampshire (1): Pierce

New Jersey (1): Cleveland

Pennsylvania (1): Buchanan

Texas (1): Lyndon B. Johnson

Vermont (1): Coolidge

Washington, D. C. (1): Wilson

Vice Presidents Elevated

Fourteen Vice Presidents rose to the office of President. The list below includes the Vice Presidents that became President. Their vice presidential rank and dates of service are in parentheses.

John Adams (1st, 1789-1797)

Thomas Jefferson (2nd, 1797-1801)

Martin Van Buren (8th, 1837-1841)

John Tyler (10th, 1841)

Millard Fillmore (12th, 1849-1850)

Andrew Johnson (16th, 1865-1869)

Chester A. Arthur (20th, 1881-1885)

Theodore Roosevelt (25th, 1901-1909)

Calvin Coolidge (29th, 1921-1923)

Harry S. Truman (34th, 1945)

Richard M. Nixon (36th, 1953-1961)

Lyndon B. Johnson (37th, 1861-1863)

Gerald R. Ford (40th, 1973-1974)

George H. W. Bush (43rd, 1981-1989)

Other Previous Political Experience

Most Presidents had political experience other than serving as Vice President before assuming America's highest office. This includes twenty-five who served in at least one house of Congress. The lists below include the Presidents by the political offices other than Vice President they held. Several Presidents held more than one political office.

Governors (20): Jefferson (Virginia), Monroe (Virginia), Jackson (Florida Territory), Van Buren (New York), William H. Harrison (Indiana Territory), Tyler (Virginia), Polk (Tennessee), Andrew Johnson (Tennessee and Military Governor of Tennessee), Hayes (Ohio), Cleveland (New York), McKinley (Ohio), Theodore Roosevelt (New York), Taft (Governor-General of the Philippines and Provisional Governor of Cuba), Wilson (New Jersey), Coolidge (Massachusetts), Franklin D. Roosevelt (New York), Carter (Georgia), Reagan (California), Clinton (Arkansas), George W. Bush (Texas)

US House of Representatives (19): Madison, John Quincy Adams, Jackson, William H. Harrison, Tyler, Polk, Fillmore, Pierce, Buchanan, Lincoln, Andrew Johnson, Hayes, Garfield, McKinley, Kennedy, Lyndon B. Johnson, Nixon, Ford, George H. W. Bush

US Senate (16): Monroe, John Quincy Adams, Jackson, Van Buren, William H. Harrison, Tyler, Pierce, Buchanan, Andrew Johnson, Benjamin Harrison, Harding, Truman, Kennedy, Lyndon B. Johnson, Nixon, Obama

Both the US House and the US Senate (10): John Quincy Adams, Andrew Jackson, William H. Harrison, Tyler, Pierce, Buchanan, Andrew Johnson, Kennedy, Lyndon B. Johnson, Nixon

Cabinet Members (9): Jefferson (Secretary of State), Madison (Secretary of State), Monroe (Secretary of State, Secretary of War), John Quincy Adams (Secretary of State), Van Buren (Secretary of State), Buchanan (Secretary of State), Grant (Secretary of War), Taft (Secretary of War), Hoover (Secretary of Commerce)

Ambassadors (8): John Adams (Great Britain), Jefferson (France), Monroe (France), John Quincy Adams (The Netherlands, Portugal, Prussia, Russia, Great Britain), Van Buren (Great Britain), William H. Harrison (Columbia), Buchanan (Great Britain), George H. W. Bush (The United Nations, People's Republic of China)

Continental Congress (5): Washington, John Adams, Madison, Monroe

Mayors (3): Andrew Johnson (Greenville, Tennessee), Cleveland (Buffalo, New York), Coolidge (Northampton, Massachusetts)

Other Federal Departments (1): George H. W. Bush (CIA Director)

Lawyer Presidents

Presidents have held many occupations. However, more practiced law than held any other profession. The list below includes the twenty-seven Presidents who held law degrees:

John Adams, Jefferson, Madison, Monroe, John Quincy Adams, Jackson, Van Buren, Tyler, Polk, Fillmore, Pierce, Buchanan, Lincoln, Hayes, Garfield, Arthur, Cleveland, Benjamin Harrison, McKinley, Taft, Wilson, Coolidge, Franklin D. Roosevelt, Nixon, Ford, Clinton, Obama

General Presidents

Most of America's Presidents have served in the military. Some have become famous soldiers. Twelve served as Generals. The list below contains the names and ranks of the Presidents who served as Generals.

George Washington: General of the Armies

Andrew Jackson: Major General

William H. Harrison: Major General

Zachary Taylor: Major General

Franklin Pierce: Brigadier General

Andrew Johnson: Brigadier General

Ulysses S. Grant: General of the Army

Rutherford B. Hayes: Major General

James A. Garfield: Major General

Chester A. Arthur: Brigadier General

Benjamin Harrison: Brigadier General

Dwight D. Eisenhower: General of the Army

Died in Office

The eight Presidents listed below died in office. The list includes the Presidents who died in office and the years of their deaths.

William H. Harrison (1841)

Zachary Taylor (1850)

Abraham Lincoln (1865)

James A. Garfield (1881)

William McKinley (1901)

Warren G. Harding (1923)

Franklin D. Roosevelt (1945)

John F. Kennedy (1963)

Assassinated

The list below is of the four assassinated Presidents and the years of their deaths.

Abraham Lincoln (1865)

James A. Garfield (1881)

William McKinley (1901)

John F. Kennedy (1963)

Locales Named for Presidents

There have been many places named for American Presidents. The towns and cities named for Presidents number into several hundred. This being the case, the author chose not to include them here. Instead, the author lists state capitals, counties, national capitals, and states named for Presidents.

Presidents with state capitals named for them (4):

Thomas Jefferson – Jefferson City, Missouri

James Madison – Madison, Wisconsin

Andrew Jackson – Jackson, Mississippi

Abraham Lincoln – Lincoln, Nebraska

Presidents with counties named for them (23):

George Washington (31 counties)

Thomas Jefferson (26 counties)

Andrew Jackson (22 counties)

Abraham Lincoln (16 counties)

Ulysses S. Grant (12 counties)

James K. Polk (11 counties)

John Adams (8 counties)

James A. Garfield (6 counties)

Martin Van Buren (4 counties)

William H. Harrison (4 counties)

Zachary Taylor (4 counties)

Franklin Pierce (4 counties)

John Quincy Adams (3 counties)

James Buchanan (3 counties)

John Tyler (2 counties)

Millard Fillmore (2 counties)

Grover Cleveland (2 counties)

Theodore Roosevelt (2 counties)

Rutherford B. Hayes (1 county)

William McKinley (1 county)

Benjamin Harrison (1 county)

Chester A. Arthur (1 county)

Warren G. Harding (1 county)

Presidents with National Capitals named for them (2):

George Washington – Washington D. C.

James Monroe – Monrovia, Liberia

States named for Presidents (1):

George Washington – Washington State

Minority Presidents

A "minority President" is who wins a presidential election, but fails to win a majority of the popular vote. Since 1824, nineteen elections have resulted in the election of a minority President. Below is a list of the minority Presidents – sorted by popular vote percentage from lowest to highest. The year of the election is in parentheses.

John Quincy Adams (1824): 30.92%

Abraham Lincoln (1860): 39.65%

Bill Clinton (1992): 43.01%

Richard M. Nixon (1968): 43.42%

Woodrow Wilson (1912): 41.83%

James Buchanan (1856): 45.29%

Donald Trump (2016): 45.94%

Grover Cleveland (1892): 46.02%

Zachary Taylor (1848): 47.28%

Benjamin Harrison (1888): 47.80%

George W. Bush (2000): 47.87%

Rutherford B. Hayes (1876): 47.92%

James A. Garfield (1880): 48.31%

Grover Cleveland (1884): 48.85%

Bill Clinton (1996): 49.23%

Woodrow Wilson (1916): 49.25%

James K. Polk (1844): 49.54%

Harry S. Truman (1948): 49.55%

John F. Kennedy (1960): 49.72%

Grover Cleveland, Woodrow Wilson, and Bill Clinton were the only persons elected as minority Presidents twice.

Presidents Who "Lost" The Popular Vote

America chooses its Presidents by the vote of the Electoral College and not by the total popular vote. Sometimes a candidate wins election to the presidency, yet finishes second in the total popular vote cast. Below is a list of the five Presidents who won election while finishing second in the popular vote:

John Quincy Adams, 1824

Rutherford B. Hayes. 1876

Benjamin Harrison, 1888

George W. Bush, 2000

Donald Trump, 2016

Number of Elections Won

Below the Presidents are ranked by the number of presidential elections each won. One will notice that five Presidents never won a presidential election.

Franklin D. Roosevelt (4): 1932, 1936, 1940, 1944

George Washington (2): 1789, 1792

Thomas Jefferson (2): 1800, 1804

James Madison (2): 1808, 1812

James Monroe (2): 1816, 1820

Andrew Jackson (2): 1828, 1832

Abraham Lincoln (2): 1860, 1864

Ulysses S. Grant (2): 1868, 1872

Grover Cleveland (2): 1884, 1892

William McKinley (2): 1896, 1900

Woodrow Wilson (2): 1912, 1916

Dwight D. Eisenhower (2): 1952, 1956

Richard M. Nixon (2): 1968, 1972

Ronald Reagan (2): 1980, 1984

Bill Clinton (2): 1992, 1996

George W. Bush (2): 2000, 2004

Barack Obama (2): 2008, 2012

John Adams (1): 1796

John Quincy Adams (1): 1824

Martin Van Buren (1): 1836

William H. Harrison (1): 1840

James K. Polk (1): 1844

Zachary Taylor (1): 1848

Franklin Pierce (1): 1852

James Buchanan (1): 1856

Rutherford B. Hayes (1): 1876

James A. Garfield (1): 1880

Benjamin Harrison (1): 1888

Theodore Roosevelt (1): 1904

William H. Taft (1): 1908

Warren G. Harding (1): 1920

Calvin Coolidge (1): 1924

Herbert Hoover (1): 1928

Harry S. Truman (1): 1948

John F. Kennedy (1): 1960

Lyndon B. Johnson (1): 1964

Jimmy Carter (1): 1976

George H. W. Bush (1): 1988

Donald Trump (1): 2016

John Tyler (0):

Millard Fillmore (0)

Andrew Johnson (0)

Chester A. Arthur (0)

Gerald R. Ford (0)

Nobel Peace Prize Winners

The Nobel Peace Prize is one of the most prestigious international awards. Three sitting Presidents and one former President have won the award. The four are:

Theodore Roosevelt (1906)

Woodrow Wilson (1919)

Jimmy Carter (2002)

Barack Obama (2009)

Left-Handed Presidents

Eight American Presidents were left-handed. They were:

James A. Garfield

Herbert Hoover

Harry S. Truman

Gerald R. Ford

Ronald Reagan

George H. W. Bush

Bill Clinton

Barack Obama

Three Presidents in One Year

Twice in American history, three persons have held the office of President in the same calendar year. They were:

1861: Martin Van Buren, William H. Harrison, and John Tyler

1881: Rutherford B. Hayes, James A. Garfield, and Chester A. Arthur

Presidents who declined a Salary

Only three Americans have declined their presidential salary. They include:

Herbert Hoover (1929-1933)

John F. Kennedy (1961-1963)

Donald Trump (2017-Present)

About the Author

CL Gammon has had a life-long fascination with American History and with the written word. These joint fascinations have led to his becoming an award winning and an internationally known bestselling author of more than thirty books. Gammon, who studied Political Science at Tennessee Technological University and History and Government at Hillsdale College, has entertained and educated readers for more than a decade. Several universities, including the State University of New York and the University of Akron, have used his books as course material. In addition, articles written by Gammon have appeared in several national publications and he is currently a frequent contributor to the *American Third Party Report*. Gammon lives in Lafayette, Tennessee with his family.

Other Books by CL Gammon

CL Gammon has written books covering many topics including history, politics, sports, and fiction. They include:

Abraham Lincoln: Warrior in Chief

Alexander Hamilton's Plan for America

America's First Rules of War

America's Other Party: A Brief History of the Prohibition Party

Bad Football Saturday's 50 Worst Teams Ever!

Bizarre Murders in Tennessee: 13 True Stories

Expelling the Senate's Gentlemen Traitors

Guns, Politics and Independence

Hail to the Chief: The Presidency by the Numbers

Hanging the Macon County Witch

Jefferson Davis Rallies the Rebels (1863)

Make Sure You are Right, then Go Ahead and other Essays

McGovern-Eagleton '72: A Crazy Train Wreck

Nazi Mad Science I: High Altitude Experiments

Seven Candidates for President in 1972

Simon the Accuser: A Christian Novel

The Big Fire (A novel)

The Continental Congress: America's Forgotten Government

The Great Mormon War of 1857-1858

The Great New Hampshire Primary Myth

The Hampton Roads Conference

The Macon County Race War

The Philosophy of the Confederate Constitution

The Politics of the Crucifixion

The Preamble of the United States Constitution

The Story of the First Continental Congress

The True Story of Axis Sally

Was Lucille Ball a Communist?

Why Johnson Created the Warren Commission

Why the Articles of Confederation Failed

Printed in Great Britain
by Amazon